M000035036

Movin' Mountains

Deanna Cook Shue

Copyright © 2021 Deanna Cook Shue
All rights reserved
First Edition

NEWMAN SPRINGS PUBLISHING
320 Broad Street
Red Bank, NJ 07701

First originally published by Newman Springs Publishing 2021

Photo credit for the front cover: Whitney Dena' Photography

ISBN 978-1-63692-389-5 (Paperback)
ISBN 978-1-63692-390-1 (Digital)

Printed in the United States of America

To my precious husband, Tim, who has been by my side every step of the way and shown me the true meaning of love

To my mama, Nancy, who raised me in a Christian home and taught me the importance of faith and believing in myself

To our children and grandbabies, Dustin, Leslie, Kendal, Amber, Brett, Megan, Lane, Dylan, Paisley, and Allie, for bringing happiness into our world

Faith can move mountains.

—Matthew 17:20

Retirement? How did I get here so soon? After thirty years in the elementary classroom, I turned in my keys, ready to take on the world.

My husband, Tim, and I bought a new camper with the plan of having no plans. Sounds perfect, right? Our idea was to hit the road and go wherever it led us, stay however long we felt like staying, and do whatever we wanted to do. Then move on to the next place and do the same. We would return home whenever we were ready.

As things sometimes go, our plan of having no plans did not go as we had hoped.

In 2016, I retired on October 1. On November 2, I had a stroke. Around Christmas, I was diagnosed with cancer. Happy retirement to me!

Here is our story.

"Bye! I love you!"

"I love you, babe! I'll see you when you get back."

I remember this day so vividly. Tim was working in the yard as I was leaving to get my haircut. He was mowing the grass, planting flowers, making it look beautiful. I could not wait to get back and see the charm he was adding to our home.

Little did we know at that time that our simple world was about to change.

Before entering the heavier traffic behind the mall, I glanced over to the right as I was passing Country Club Drive. As soon as I did, I felt something pop beside my left eye. It was really strange. All of the sudden, things started blurring. I saw a kaleidoscope of colors—red, blue, green, purple, yellow—all swirling round and round. It was scaring me.

"Please, God, don't let me hit anybody. Please don't let anybody hit me!"

My heart was beating out of my chest. I was fighting back the tears and trying to keep my head on straight so I could think how to get my car off the road. By that time, I was in the middle of the busy mall traffic surrounded by lots of cars. Well, actually, lots of "colors" because that is really all I could make out around me. I knew I had to get my car off the road and quick; however, my vision was so cloudy that I could not see an entrance to turn into anywhere.

God, please, please, please don't let me hit anybody! Please don't let anybody hit me! O God, please don't let me hurt anybody.

With everything happening so quickly and not having a clue what was happening to me, I was getting more frightened by the minute. My heart began beating more rapidly. More forcefully. Where was I going to go? What was I going to do?

I remembered there was a stoplight not too far down the road. In my mind, if I could just make it to that light, I could turn right and pull up into the mall parking lot.

As I safely approached the light, I thanked God that I made it. Even though it was blurry, I knew it was red. When it turned green, I started moving slowly. Before approaching the parking lot, I could tell that there was a big, wide-open space on my right, and even though I had traveled that road many times before, I had never paid attention to it. I carefully pulled in and stopped.

My vision had gotten so bad that I could not even see the numbers on my phone to call Tim. Thank God for Siri because that was the only way I could call him. As I started to try to explain what was going on, he asked me where I was, but I could not tell him. I had no idea what the place was called. All I could tell him was that I was behind a brick building. Obviously, my mind was not thinking clearly, and my speech was becoming more garbled.

He immediately jumped into his truck and headed straight there. He was able to find me by what little I was able to tell him. As I waited on him, I could tell things were getting worse. My body began feeling really strange. Not only was everything blurry, I had begun seeing double. Thank goodness we do not live that far from where I was, so he got to me quickly.

By the time he arrived, my condition had worsened. He could barely understand anything that I was trying to say and knew he had to get me to the emergency room, which fortunately was right next door to where we were.

He learned quickly as he tried to put me in his truck that I could not stand up by myself. He had to help me make the transition.

Thinking back, I should have called 911 first. Having the paramedics there working with me would have been better than calling Tim first. Since then, we have learned that valuable lesson.

Before I go any further, I want to share the most important part of this story that happened between Country Club Drive and the parking lot that I safely pulled into. Remember, I was in busy mall traffic. You see, it was not me driving my car that day; it was God. There is no doubt in my mind. Let me say that again: *God was driving my car!* Let that sink in a minute. There was absolutely no way I could have made it through the danger of that traffic alone without hitting another car, the curb, or a sign. He showed out big-time and, boy, we were glad He did! His protecting me that day was the first of many miracles that He would be doing in my life in the following years.

Now back to the story. As soon as we arrived at the emergency room, the nurses started working with me. Tim had to do all the paperwork and sign everything because, of course, I could not see, speak clearly, or even stand by myself. I was like a limp dishrag.

After having multiple tests, we got the news that no one thinks will happen to them. We learned that I had a stroke in the major part of my brain that affected my sight, speech, and mobility. This day was getting scarier.

"You've had a stroke."

Those words were not an easy pill to swallow. *How could that be?* I thought I was healthy. What caused it? The only answer was a small blood clot went to my brain. What caused the blood clot? There was no answer. That made things even scarier because then we knew something was going on inside my body but we had no idea what. What if it happens again? When would it happen? What if I am driving again when it does?

After being admitted to the hospital and spending the next couple of days with what seemed like every specialist on the payroll, I could see, talk, and walk normally again! Fortunately, there was no residual from the stroke.

Thank you, God! You've done it again!

Twice in one week! He kept me safe on the road and healed me from this very alarming situation that could have ended much differently. Thanks to Him, I was going home to live my life without any residual from the stroke.

Almost two months later…

What in the world? My stomach was getting bigger and bigger. I knew I had not been eating very healthy, but in no way did I realize I had been eating like a pig—or at least that was what I looked like! I felt like I had been gaining weight for a while, but this was different. Something was seriously not right. It really started bothering me.

One evening, the day after Christmas, I felt something really weird. I immediately went to Tim and told him to feel the top of my stomach. It looked and felt like I was pregnant. You read that right. It looked and felt like I was *pregnant*! My stomach was hard and pooched out as if I were going to give birth within a few months. No way. I was fifty-one years old, we had raised four beautiful children, and we had four precious grandbabies. Oh yeah, did I mention I had had my tubes tied, snipped, burnt, all of the above? Maybe not *all* of the above, but you get my drift. Nope! No way I could be pregnant! Stomach problems? Digestive problems? We decided to call my primary care physician, Dr. Levy, the next morning.

Before making that call, I looked at my stomach again and could not believe what I was seeing. Yes, it still pooched out. Yes, it was still hard to press on, but *what*? You have got to be kidding me! There was a vein running up my stomach—just like when you are pregnant! What in the world was going on?

Dr. Levy, who I have seen and trusted for years, was not in the office that day, so I was scheduled with his nurse practitioner, Lindsey, whom I had never met. I was nervous about that in the beginning but in the long run she definitely gets credit. She is a huge part of saving my life, doing all the right things to get us the answers we needed to begin this long, crazy journey. We are forever grateful to her!

I am sure that you did not choose this book to read "too much information," but there must be some of that to tell my story. Believe me, there will be more later. On my first visit with Lindsey, she told me I was "stopped up" and needed to use the bathroom. She said we would start with the least abrasive treatment. I followed the instructions she gave me. It was not helping, plus I began having a few pains.

The following week on Tuesday, I went back to see her again. She sent me to the hospital the following day to have a CT scan so we could get a better understanding of what was going on. Things were getting serious. The scan went smoothly, and before long, Tim and I were on our way home.

In *less than an hour* of arriving home, my phone rang. It was my doctor's office. Dr. Levy, the doctor I mentioned earlier whom I have seen and trusted for years, wanted me to come into his office that afternoon so he could discuss the results of my scan. *What?* There was no way this could be good! I was terrified. The tears started flowing, and I began shaking all over. Lying on my bed, about every thought you could think of ran through my mind.

Oh, what a visit. Tim, my mama, and I sat silently in the waiting room, waiting for my name to be called. My heart was beating out of my chest. They did not say, but I bet theirs were too. We could only imagine what we were about to face.

"Deanna."

There it was. My name. Was this real? Was this really happening? Did I really have to go back and hear what they were going to tell me?

The three of us followed the nurse into my doctor's room to wait for him. After just a minute or two, in walked another nurse along with Dr. Levy and Lindsey. Oh, I knew it was not going to be good. They had never paraded into the room that way.

Dr. Levy began to share the results of the scan. There was a growth, the size of a regular-size envelope, on my ovary. It was huge.

My eyes filled with tears as I listened, even though I was trying so hard not to cry. Tim stood strong by my side, rubbing my back as we were getting the news, while my mama stood close by him. Then, there it was…the word we did not want to hear; the word that, again, nobody thinks will happen to them.

"There is a possibility that it is ovarian cancer, but we will not know for sure till after you have surgery."

"Well, don't people die from this?"

"Yes, they do."

I burst into tears. Tim wrapped his arms around me. My sweet mama wrapped her arms around us both. We all cried. I remember feeling numb. Dr. Levy, who was so respectful, let us have our time. I only cried for about two or three minutes. I knew I had to get myself together.

"Where do we go from here? What do we do to make me better?"

I knew the sooner we got started, the sooner I would be okay. Again, he stated that we would not be sure it was cancer till after the surgery. I knew. There was no doubt in my mind. I knew the doctors had seen enough to know if a growth was cancer or not, especially when the tumor was as big as mine. What would happen next?

Before the appointment that afternoon, Dr. Levy, who is the best doctor ever, had already planned for me to see a top-notch oncologist the next day. The appointment had been scheduled so I would not have to wait for answers. He finished listening to our concerns and answering our questions. Of course, we really did not know what to ask at that time. We had stepped into the unknown. Our world had just been turned upside down.

We left his office. I felt like I walked in one person and came out another. I was so confused. How could this be happening? It did not seem real. I felt like my mind was in a fog.

On the way to our cars, my mama asked if we wanted her to go with us to tell our kids. Tell our kids? What? I had to wrap my own head around it before I could share it with anybody else, even our kids! A million thoughts were racing through my mind. I did not want to die! I wanted to live! I wanted to see our last two children get married and meet all of our grandchildren! I wanted to know them, and I wanted them to know me! I wanted to grow old with my husband and rock on the front porch in our rocking chairs like we had always planned! How could this be happening?

As we were leaving the parking lot, that moment of anger struck. I burst into tears again, balled up my fist, and hit the door of the truck. Hard.

"Why is this happening?"

As soon as I said that, I knew it was wrong. I knew not to ask *why*. I knew God had a reason. He has a reason for everything.

My words then changed to asking what the reason could possibly be.

"God, what do I do with this?"

Do not get me wrong. I was still upset, but the anger subsided.

When I had calmed down, I remember Tim looking at me so sweetly and saying, "You know we need to tell the kids."

I took a deep breath and said, "Let's do it."

I knew I had to get myself together so we could do what needed to be done. I wanted them to hear it from us. Although I was not feeling it at the moment, I had always been a strong person. I knew that I had to pull every bit of strength I had in me to tell them. I was scared that the more upset they saw me, the more upset they would be.

All four of our children are grown and live on their own. We thought it would be best to go to each one of them personally to tell them. Tim called each one to make sure they were home so we could drop by.

Each one had their own reaction while trying to be strong for me.

Personally, I know how hard it was for us to tell our adult children. With that in mind, I can only imagine explaining it to our little ones. Our sons and their wives, Dustin and Leslie and Kendal and Amber have done a wonderful job talking to our grandbabies about it. Yes, it is a whole different level of explanation, but it still had to be dealt with. They had to let them know that Gramsie would look different. She will not have any hair. She will not be able to run around with you like she did because she will be tired. She will have to go to the doctor and the hospital a lot. No matter what, she loves you more than ever. I do not know their exact words or what all they told them, but I do know the grandbabies have handled it well thanks to their mommies and daddies.

Deanna and Tim are surrounded by the love of their children and grandbabies. L to R: Row 1-Deanna, Tim; Row 2-Paisley, Lane, Dylan, Allie; Row 3-Dustin, Leslie, Brett, Megan, Kendal, Amber Photo Credit: Whitney Dena' Photography

I do not remember much about what happened after we got home from making our rounds that night except crying and telling God I knew He had a reason and asking Him to please show it to me. I remember telling Him I was not asking why, but please, *please* show me what He wanted me to do with the information we were just given.

Looking back across time, I realized so many things happened that prepared me for this moment.

Most important was my personal relationship with Jesus. For years, I had been growing closer to Him—my faith growing stronger, my commitment getting deeper. I trusted Him with my whole heart. I knew He had a plan for my life. I trusted His will.

The way I just wrote that sounds like it is all in the past. That could not be further from the truth. I am still very much growing in my relationship with Him every single day.

Another thing. Years ago, my precious daddy passed away in a freak accident. In fact, I had just hung up the phone after speaking with him when it happened. You can only imagine what kind of mind frame our family was in. We were all in shock. The night of his viewing, a lady came up to me and said—I will never forget this, "You shouldn't ask God why. Why not? Why shouldn't it have been your daddy?"

Oh. My. Goodness! I was livid! How in the world could she have the nerve to say something like that to me at that time when my whole world was just ripped apart? I still feel that way about her timing; however, when I was diagnosed, that memory came back to me. Why not me? There was a reason. There was a reason it was me.

Looking back to the week I received my diagnosis, it was such a blur. I saw the nurse practitioner on Tuesday; had a scan on Wednesday; met my oncologist, Dr. Miller, on Thursday; and had a hysterectomy first thing Friday morning. I discovered how blessed I was that everything happened so fast because I later learned that some people in my situation have to wait for weeks to get their appointments. I am so thankful that we were able to move quickly.

From the moment we met Dr. Miller, my husband, my mama, and I all felt very comfortable with her. She was personable and clear in her explanations. We knew we were in good hands. I sure was glad because first thing the next morning, she would be cutting my abdomen open and taking parts out. When someone is about to do that, you definitely want to feel comfortable with them.

God and I did a lot of talking that evening after our visit with her, as we had that whole week. This cancer thing was new to us. I am not going to lie: I was scared. It was the fear of the unknown, fear of everything swirling around me at top speed. It was all happening so fast, like a whirlwind.

After my hysterectomy, Dr. Miller explained to my family that the cancer had spread to my lymph nodes. This gave me a diagnosis of ovarian cancer stage 3C. We found out that not only do I have one kind of cancer but two mixed together. Both are rare and aggressive.

Thankfully, she believed she got it all except the tiny masses in my lymph nodes that I would be getting chemotherapy for in the following weeks. Stage 3 was definitely a concern to me—it was too close to stage 4; however, I knew that, whatever happened, God was in control.

This was the first of many hospital stays. I tried to get Tim to go home and get some rest, but he would not. He slept night after night in that cramped recliner set up in the room for guests. The nurses really liked him because he took care of my every need except the medical side of it, which they had to do. I remember looking over at him sleeping in that chair thinking that this was what true love looked like.

Deanna and Tim are spending time together in the hospital before he falls asleep in the recliner that will be his bed for the next several nights.

When we left the hospital, Tim and I went to his parents' house to stay for a bit so that Mary, my mother-in-law, could help with my care. Get-well cards started coming daily with well wishes and sometimes gift cards for meals. People prepared tasty meals for our family. I received devotional books to help with my journey and many other thoughtful gifts.

Tim's parents, Mary and Colon, are dancing the
night away at their granddaughter's wedding.

I was amazed at the outpouring of support, from close family
and friends to people I have not known long, to people I have not
seen in years, people from in town and out of town. The love was
bubbling over. Most of all, there were lots and lots of prayers coming
our way.

Knowing the power of prayer, I immediately said, "Yes!" when
my mama suggested being anointed.

I wanted that very much. The choice was to either have it done
at church or have our preacher come to the house. I wanted it done
at church because I wanted to invite people close to me. The more
prayers, the better. I talked to our preacher and told him it would be
family and a few friends.

The evening I was to be anointed, we were running a little late
getting to the church.

Ring, ring.

"Deanna, there are fifty plus people here and they're still coming! Let's get more of a plan together!"

Ha! That was our preacher, Scott. I told him that my mama
always said when I do something, I do it big! We had talked earlier

about what we wanted to do but did not have a formal plan. It was just a small get-together, and I would be anointed. We added a few more details to the first plan, and everything went great.

The best part of the night? When I saw my brother, who did not, would not, go to church at the time, walk through those doors and sit down at the back of the church. I went back there, hugged him, and asked him if he wanted to move up front with everybody else. He told me no, that he would just sit back there. He told me he was there to support me, that he would not have missed it for the world. As soon as it was over, he did not stay around to talk. He left, but knowing he was there for me meant everything.

Not long after that, I would be starting chemo. I wondered which side effects I would have to deal with. Which ones would happen to me? How bad would they be? Will I lose my hair? All of it? I hoped I would not be throwing up all day, every day. Ugh. That would have been awful. Luckily, the side effects of the first round of chemo were not that bad—not good, but not that bad.

The one side effect I dreaded the most came way too soon for me. I am not a vain person but, man, I did not want to lose my hair. One of my sisterfriends, Wende, is my hairstylist. She had a good plan. Because I had never in my life even had short hair, she suggested we cut off a little at a time to help me get used to it, and when I was ready, she would shave it off. We went with the plan. She took me shopping for wigs and turned what was a gloomy time for me into a fun time. She made me laugh and kept my spirits high. She even went as far as to buy one of the wigs for me.

Before long, my hair started falling out on its own. Oh my goodness. It was real. I really was going to be bald. Strands of hair started coming out little by little, then by the handfuls. I cried for days, trying to hold on to my hair as long as I could. I did not want it shaved! I did not want to be bald! I did not want to lose my hair!

One afternoon, I jumped into the shower before going to dinner with my friend, Debbie. Handfuls, and I mean handfuls, of hair came out in clumps and it was not stopping. I stood in the shower and bawled like a baby. I knew the time had come that I dreaded so desperately. I called Wende and explained to her what was happening. I told her that I had to do it while I had the nerve. She told me to come to her shop that night after they closed and she would do it then. I was so scared. I could not quit crying.

Debbie and I went on to dinner. This helped keep my mind occupied till we had to be at the shop. Sitting in the restaurant, she kept my spirits high on the surface. Inside, I knew what was coming.

A little before the appointment, we left and headed that way. Tim met us there. The four of us were gathered as the hair came off. I tried so hard not to cry but I could not help it. That was seriously one of the hardest things I had ever done in my life. I cried harder and longer then than when I heard my diagnosis. We all cried. I came home and cried some more. In fact, I have tears leaking out of my eyes as I am writing this because of the memories of the horrible feelings I had that night.

Wigs, scarves, hats—I tried them all. I wore them a couple of times, but I never felt comfortable. Truthfully, I felt like I was dressed up for Halloween when wearing the wigs and I felt like I looked sick when I wore the scarves or hats. I just did not feel like me.

Who is that lady in the wig? Oh! It is Deanna with her son, Brett.

Tim and I, along with our son, Kendal, and his kids, went to the beach for a weekend. I kept something on my head that trip because, at the time, no one other than the four people I mentioned earlier had seen me bald. Eventually, I got up the courage—and, boy, did it take courage—and walked into the living room with my bald head shining! It was then that I heard some of the most precious words come out of our son's mouth.

"You look more like yourself with nothing on your head."

That may not sound like a big deal to some people, but to me, it gave me the boost of confidence I needed.

Shortly thereafter, I decided to take a trip to a local retail shop alone and…bald. It was the first time I had ever gone in public that way. Talk about courage! Even though I am sure no one there gave a flying flip about what I looked like, I felt self-conscious as if people were staring straight at me. I had never felt that way in my life before then.

Let me tell you what happened while I was there. One of the salesclerks stepped into my path, looked me directly in the eyes, and said, "You are beautiful."

Again, I began to cry and explained to her the whole story.

"You are out in public now around total strangers. When you get back home, you have family and friends that love and support you. God is going to give you the courage you need to go out just like you want to go out."

I heard Him loud and clear. That was God. He put that lady in my path, a complete stranger, to remind me that He had me, that He is always by my side taking care of me—even over something like my hair. He knew my struggles and knew exactly what I needed.

From that time on, I let my bald shine! Believe me, it was still not easy in the beginning. In fact, a little funny here: when we went out, I would always ask my husband the same question. "How do I look?"

I mean, really, how many different ways can a lady look when she is bald? Like I was going to look better one way or the other. Bald is bald. He always answered me with the sweetest voice and a loving smile on his face.

Now this is one expensive hair do! Deanna
is showing her new look!

Tim, Brett, and Megan are sharing a special outing with Deanna.
This is the first time she went out in their hometown with
nothing on her head. Yep! She is rockin' her baldness in public!

"You look beautiful."

What else would he say?

Our grandbabies all had different reactions when they saw me with no hair. To lighten the situation, I told them that every time they hugged me that it would make my hair grow a little more. The girls were young enough to believe it. The boys were a couple of years older, so I am not sure if they believed it or if they just played along. Either way, I got lots of hugs while my hair was growing out!

Deanna and Tim's granddaughters are helping their gramsie's hair grow by giving her hugs and kisses.

My bald head was not the only thing I covered when the side effects first started. Imagine every night before going to bed, you have to put a thick layer of lotion on your feet and hands and then cover them with white cotton socks and gloves to wear while you sleep. This is what I had to do to help keep my skin healthy and try to avoid it from cracking and peeling. Night after night. Lotion. Socks. Lotion. Gloves. This got old, especially since I do not like anything on my feet while I sleep. I quickly learned I did not like anything on my hands either.

Now imagine—no more hot showers, which I love. Doing the dishes, which did not hurt my feelings, were out of the question. Doing either would burn my skin. I, as they say, had to "test the water" in the shower. I would turn it a little warmer and then a little warmer, trying to find a comfortable temperature. Luckily, I was able to settle on a temperature with a little warmth without it burning my skin, but boy, was it an energy zapper! Because taking a shower used all of my strength, I had to start using a shower chair. This was the only way I could get through it without being totally exhausted.

Exhausted. That seems to be a pretty common word when you are going through chemotherapy. Need to sleep. Gotta sleep. Sleep for hours. Fatigue. That is a biggie during chemo. Trying to clean? Want to play with your grandbabies? Plan to go out with family or friends? On the days you are feeling really tired, you might as well stay home and hit the bed because if you go out, you will be turning around soon to come back home and do what you should have done in the first place. Go to bed. You have to do what your body tells you. When your body says sleep, you sleep. I would sleep for hours and hours, day after day. Literally.

Think about dragging through a long, hard day at work and then coming home and taking care of your family. You cannot wait to get in your bed. Now, multiply that times ten—no, twenty—ah, go ahead and multiply it by a hundred. You cannot stay awake. In the beginning, I slept all the time. I could be wide awake one minute and dozing off the next. My eyes would be so heavy that I could not hold them open. There are many times, still, that I will fall asleep while sitting up on the couch. Tim will wake me so I can go to bed.

With cancer patients, you can hear some gross stories. People are always hugging the toilet throwing up when they are on chemo. They are throwing up so much that they have nothing left inside of them and begin dry-heaving. Some people throw up on and off all day long. You even hear of patients throwing up when they are at the infusion lab. I had heard all the horror stories above plus more about throwing up on chemo and, boy, was I dreading it. Throwing up is what I call "cancer sick." That last one really got to me because I could not imagine sitting in the lab for hours getting my infusion while hearing people throw up around me, not to mention the smell. Ooooh, it grosses me out just thinking about it. Can you imagine the chain reaction and those poor nurses having to clean up all that mess? By the way, that never happened while I was there. Thank God!

Luckily, I was not one of the people that it affected that way. On my journey, I have only been "cancer sick" a day and a half. That was it. A day and a half. Dr. Miller taught me how to manage it from the beginning, and I have not had to deal with it anymore. I have been nauseous some, but not actually "cancer sick."

If you are going through this and you are wondering about her advice, she prescribed me two kinds of medication for nausea. She told me to get the one in my system before I went to the hospital for my infusion. Once there, they gave me another type through my port before the actual chemo drug. Then after I went home, I was to alternate the two meds she prescribed. She said not to wait till I felt sick. Start taking them before that. I followed her directions and got along fine.

At my very first appointment, she said that everybody is different, and the chemo will affect each person differently. I held on to that, convincing myself that just because a side effect happened to someone else did not mean it was going to happen to me.

Not only does the chemo cause a person to lose the hair on their head, they lose it everywhere else on their body—eyelashes, eyebrows—yes, everywhere.

Having said this, my nose would constantly run, like water dripping, but I was not sick. Someone, I do not remember who, told me it was because I had no nose hairs to stop it, that when I lost my hair, I lost my nose hair too. Hmmm, made sense to me. Whoever would have thought of losing your nose hair? We should have bought stock in tissues!

Even though losing my hair was one of the hardest things I have ever had to go through, there was actually a good side to it. The chemo also stopped it from growing on my legs, so I did not have to shave them!

Chemo can have so many different effects on your body. From the very beginning, Dr. Miller told us if my temperature reached 100.4, I was to go to the emergency room.

The first time this happened, off we went, not having any idea what we were about to face.

During my first of several hospital stays with cancer, it ended up that I had pneumonia, neutropenia, and sepsis—all caused by the chemo I was receiving. It was not looking good.

The main things I remember about that stay was that they had to remove the flowers from my room and I could not eat fresh fruit—all because I was neutropenic.

Tim took my flowers to the nurses' station for them to enjoy.

At the time, I did not know how dangerous sepsis was. I learned afterward. What I do know is that God kept me alive. I could have very easily left this earth during that hospital stay.

The side effects were not that bad during my first round of chemo, except for that one particular hospital scare. Sure, we had to deal with some things: the hospital visits; the hair—oh, the hair, that was terrible; and the fatigue. But other than that, we felt like it went pretty well. I stayed focused on the fact that it could have definitely been a whole lot worse.

One of the hardest things for me was not being able to go out and do what I wanted to, considering I am one of those people who has always been on the go. We had to watch who I interacted with. If we knew somebody was sick, even with a cold, we could not go around them. If there was going to be a massive group of people somewhere, we would not go, especially during my NADIR period, which was when my white blood cell count was low, making it easiest for me to become ill. In other words, we were more or less living the "quarantine life" before it was mandated during this COVID crisis.

We were so excited when the first round of treatments were over and everything looked fine! I could get back to living a normal life that did not involve doctor visits two or three times a week, getting chemotherapy drugs infused into my body, staying home during the NADIR period, sleeping all the time, or being concerned about what side effect might pop up next.

When I was through, Dr. Miller gave me a certificate that stated I had completed the treatments. I was beaming! I made it! I was so proud—you would have thought I had just graduated with another degree! In front of the giant pineapple fountain outside of the hospital, I proudly held up my certificate as Tim took pictures! Finally, that mess was over, and I could get back to living my life before that awful C word decided to move in on me. That was on a Monday in May.

On the following Friday, I was able to spend the weekend in the woods doing one of my favorite things ever. As I had done for years, I volunteered at Camp LUCK (Lucky Unlimited Cardiac Kids), a camp that serves kids with heart disease. This happened to be our family camp, so parents and siblings were also there bringing on the excitement. They were amazed that I was able to go after finishing chemo only four days earlier. As long as it was in my control, there would be no stopping me from going to camp. At the end of a very fulfilling weekend, they presented me with a beautiful bouquet of red flowers and a Bravery and Courage Award! Our camp family is awesome!

Mark, Amanda, Karime, Carley, and Porter are celebrating Deanna's Bravery and Courage Award given to her by her Camp LUCK family for finishing her first set of chemo treatments.

After a little time had passed, our neighborhood was smelling good as Tim used the big smoker in the backyard to cook some of his delicious award-winning BBQ, baked beans, squash and onions, and potatoes and carrots so we could have a big ol' celebration to commemorate the departure of that ugly disease! Thanks to family and friends, we had every kind of dessert you could possibly think of. People came from near and far. In fact, a couple of different people counted and said there were over two hundred people there.

There was so much love in the room that night. People were seeing family and friends they had not seen in a while. Lots of smiles. Tons of hugs. Hundreds of pictures taken. I wish I had been able to spend time with all of them so they would know how much I appreciated them supporting our family. I did my best to get around to as many people as I could.

Fast-forward three months to August. I went back to Camp LUCK. This time, it was Kids' Camp; only the heart kids and one of their siblings would be staying with us. On Sunday afternoon, when the gates opened, our campers came running in with giant smiles as they hugged all the familiar faces while their parents were loaded down carrying luggage—suitcases, trunks, drawers, bags, boxes, fans; you name it, they had it—to leave their children with us for a week. Some parents had experienced this steamy August heat before (this was not their first rodeo) and had learned that bringing a wagon to haul their gear in made the move-in life a lot easier.

The days followed with our heart kids experiencing activities that other children did. They were there for the week of their lives, and that was just what we gave them—rock climbing, arts and crafts, dances, gaga ball, hot-air balloon rides (tethered, of course), sailing, canoeing, rambo, athletics, swimming, jumping on the water trampoline, zip-lining; the list goes on.

After the first couple of days, I started not to feel so well. I hoped it was because of the heat. I found myself going back to our camper often for naps. Instead of staying in a cabin as most of the campers and staff did, Tim had taken our air-conditioned camper down for me to stay in.

As our loving camp family does, they would check on me to make sure I was okay and had what I needed. Even though I appreciated it very much, I did not want them worrying about me when they were there for our campers. I tried to push through, I really did. I ended up having to call Tim and have him come get me early. It broke my heart.

When we got home, I found out why I was feeling so bad. Once again, the words you never want to hear.

"The cancer is back."

I was devastated. You have got to be kidding me! I could not believe what I was hearing. I thought we were done.

Again, God, what do You want me to do with this? I know You have a plan. What is it? Please show me.

I asked this question many times over again.

Thinking back to our heart kids, I knew why I was given that opportunity. I saw the strength, the determination, the fighting side, the warrior in these kids who had spent their entire lives in doctors' offices and hospitals. They had had multiple heart surgeries, open heart surgeries, and even heart transplants, yet they were living life to the fullest! I saw no fear as they conquered new activities. They laughed. They played. They sang. They danced. They were wide open the whole time they were at camp. While I thought I was helping them learn new things, they were actually teaching me that I could get through this crazy journey I was back on. Most of them had been through way more than I could ever imagine. I knew if they could do it, I could do it.

While I am telling you about my Camp LUCK family and what they have done for me on this journey, I want to share about my other camp family from YMCA Camp Cherokee and the support they have given me.

Camp Cherokee has played a part in my life for forty-five years. Yep! You read that right—forty-five years! Starting as a camper at age ten, I was then hired as a staff member in high school. As an adult, I volunteered there for over twenty years and am now currently a Cherokee Conservation Corps member. I am telling you all of this to give you an idea of how near and dear to my heart this place is to me.

Not only does the place mean the world to me, but also my friends I have met there do too.

Every year, we have an alumni weekend where we all go back to camp and act like kids again. It is a chance to step back in time and be with our childhood friends while doing all kinds of fun camp activities.

Very much to my surprise, one of our alumni weekends was dedicated to me. The first night at dinner, our T-shirts were given out. They sported teal in support of ovarian cancer and read CHEROKEE STRONG in honor of me. On the back were words to the song that we always played last at the dances. The words were about standing united and being there for each other.

Beige, Deanna, and Laura are wearing the shirts that were made by her YMCA Camp Cherokee family in her honor.

Now, for the most important, most incredible part of the night… After we ate, my friend Mary Lawrence requested that everyone stand in a circle and hold hands so they could pray for me. I never dreamed of what was about to take place next. Going around the circle, *every one* of my Cherokee friends said a prayer for me. To say my heart melted would be an understatement. Something very special happened that night in the mess hall, something that not only affected me but affected us all. God has a way with showing up and showing out at the perfect time. This was most definitely one of those times. With His presence, the power of prayer, and the love of friends—it was a night we will always remember.

After learning that I was going to have to face this mess again, I had gone to dinner with Wende. The devastation was still fresh and new. It was definitely harder to hear the second time because I knew, or at least I *thought* I knew, what I was about to face. I did not have a clue. Not one inkling. One of the things she said to me as we sat in her car talking after dinner was this—I will never forget it and I say it to myself often:

"This is your life now."

Man, was she right! Here we are, more than four years later, and I still remind myself of what she said.

"This *is* my life now." Only now I add, "And I am living my best life. I'm going to live life to the fullest and enjoy it!"

I promised myself from the very beginning of the original diagnosis that I would not let it take me down easy—that I would fight with everything I had. I have kept that promise and I will till God sees fit to change my address to heaven.

It was time to start all over again with tests and appointments. We went for multiple tests on my organs—kidneys, liver, heart. Waiting for one. Waiting for another. The results were coming in pretty quickly, but if you are like me, you want them immediately. What seemed like a delayed wait was not actually that long. Thank God the news we received was that everything was functioning just like it was supposed to. As each result came in, we breathed a sigh of relief. We were on top of the world. Things were looking great!

Then came the tumor marker count (CA 125). It was 688. If I could add a giant-eyed emoji with a broken heart here, I would. *Six hundred eighty-eight?* Zero to 35 is normal; 50 is high…and mine was *688?* How much worse was it? Had it spread? What was going to happen to me?

The high we were on? Gone. Of course, Tim never let me know it bothered him. Instead, he encouraged me and tried to keep my spirits high while all kinds of negative thoughts were running through my mind. We learned it could go much higher; in fact, at one point mine climbed to over two thousand. I could only imagine what was going on inside my body. I was really having to give the human side of myself a talking-to and remind myself to trust God. I *knew* that He was in control and I *knew* that whatever happened was His will for my life.

At my next treatment, I was talking to my nurse navigator about my CA 125.

"You have *got* to quit putting so much emphasis on that number. There could be reasons other than the cancer that it is higher."

A couple of days later, Dr. Levy told me the same thing: "Quit putting so much emphasis on that number. There could be other things causing that."

Well, that night, I let it go. I believed them. I truly released it and thought to myself, *If there is something else, let us find out what it is and fix it.* It was actually a relief to no longer focus on it.

That same night, Tim went striper fishing out of town. He normally turned down the opportunity to go out with his friends because he did not want to leave me by myself, but this time I got him to go.

I did my normal thing after I went to bed—checked my messages, played a couple of games online, read, and went to sleep.

Well, about 4:30 in the morning, I woke up out of a sound sleep, when the most amazing thing you could ever imagine happened.

You know that feeling when you are sitting in the congregation at church and Jesus is calling you to the altar? Your heart starts beating really fast like it is about to come out of your chest; you get this eager feeling and are all excited. That woke me up!

I could hear—I promise you I am telling you the truth—*I could hear* God saying to me, "You're healed. You're healed, Deanna. I've healed you."

Oh, my goodness! That was God! He was talking to me! He has healed me! I was super pumped! It was the most incredible thing ever! It was the first time in my life that I actually *heard* Him speak to me. Oh, do not get me wrong. He has spoken to me many different times in many different ways, but this was the first time I *heard* His voice. I knew without a doubt it was *Him*! Y'all, God told me He healed me! I lay there for a minute or two soaking it all in, amazed at what had just happened.

I called Tim to share the miracle I had just witnessed. It had to scare him when he heard his phone ring that early and saw that it was me.

He quickly learned there was absolutely nothing to be scared about but a whole lot to rejoice in!

I fell back asleep, and then around 6:00, I woke up hearing Him speak to me again.

"You're healed, Deanna. I've healed you."

I wish I had the words to share my feelings with you from hearing Him tell me that—from the most loving experience ever—the words that would let you experience what I experienced that night and what I am experiencing right now. Just from thinking about it and writing about it, I have tears in my eyes—happy tears, of course. My body is tingling all over, and I have a huge smile on my face! The one thing I can tell you is that from that moment on, I knew in my heart that I was healed. I knew that I might have to go through two or three more things, maybe even nine or ten more things, but when it was all said and done, *I was healed!* There was no doubt in my mind whatsoever.

After hearing God talk to me, I had many more visits that went as cancer visits do—up and down. There was nothing like *hearing* God talk to me. No matter what information was given to me at the appointments, *He told me* He healed me. I stayed focused on that.

During one of the following visits with Dr. Miller, things felt a little different when she walked into the room. Tim was there with me, as always, when she looked me in the eye and said, "You know this is not going to get better."

I looked right back at her and responded, "My God said it is."

Boy, now I am really crying as I write. I remember that day so distinctly. I am not going to lie. This shook me up. It shook me up bad, but I could not let it get control of me. I was not giving up. God said He healed me, and I believe Him.

I know she had to tell me the "textbook version." That is what I call it, but I know that my God is stronger and mightier than anything science can throw my way. Yes, I cried. It was fiercely hard to have to hear those words. Using the word *hard* to describe hearing the woman I trust with all my heart, the woman on earth who is saving my life, say that it is not going to get better is an understatement. *Hard* does not even began to explain it. I had to keep focused on God telling me that He had healed me. I had to hold on tight to that.

After the appointment, we went to the lab so I could get my infusion. As I lay there in the recliner, tears kept sneaking down my cheeks. I was trying so hard to get it together while my precious Tim held my hand and wiped my tears.

Although the human side of the disease was showing that it did not look good, I knew my God had healed me, and I held on to that with every little bit of everything inside of me. I knew I was facing a win-win situation. I knew that whether I was healed on earth or in heaven, I won. If I were to be healed here on earth, I would be able to stay with my family. If He decided it was my time to go to heaven, I would go to live with Him. What would be greater than that?

It was that day, however, that something hit me that people should never say to a cancer patient or anyone else who is terminally ill—and it is something said all the time like it is no big deal:

"We're all going to die."

Yes, we are all going to die, but until your specialist has looked you directly in the eye and told you personally that it is not going to get any better, you have no idea how it feels. I know when people are saying that they are trying to be helpful, but it is not. Please do not ever say that to someone in this position.

It was not long before the next routine CT scan was scheduled. My nerves were a little tense that day. Okay, let me just be honest here—they were a whole lot tense. In fact, this time was one of the hardest I can remember. I *knew* God had already healed me; He had told me so, and *I believed Him*, but the human side of me was scared. I am not going to lie. The Christian side of me was reminding me to have faith, that God had already told me I was healed. I was trying my best, but the human side kept creeping in.

You see, there had been some other things going on inside my stomach. I was not sure what, but something just did not feel right. Had the cancer spread? What are they going to find? Please do not let me have to deal with anything else. Please let everything be okay. Please let them tell me the masses had shrunk. Oh, how I wish they could have given me the results right then. Waiting is the toughest part because it is so easy to let your mind wander, especially when you feel like something else is going on. I was really worried.

Shortly after the scan, on that same day, Tim and I headed for my appointment with Dr. Levy. He spoke his first words to us as he entered the room.

"Are you ready to hear some good news?"

I heard what he said, but did I hear it right? I do struggle with my hearing. What kind of good news could he have for us? To make sure I did hear him right, I had to ask, "What?"

"Do you want to hear some good news?"

"Absolutely!"

We were more than happy to take any and all good news he could throw our way.

"All three masses have shrunk. Here, look at the numbers."

Oh my goodness! They had! He could already see the results from the scan I had just an hour earlier, and it was exactly what we had prayed for! The masses were still shrinking! To me that was like God saying, "Wake up, Deanna. I told you to trust Me. Wake up." Here come the happy tears. The masses had shrunk; therefore, no spreading! Thank You, God! Thank You! Thank You! Thank You!

On the way home, I was quiet, for a short distance anyway. Reflecting on the news we just heard but more importantly on how God keeps His promises to us, I was getting more and more excited. The further we went, the faster my heart was beating. I was getting that jumpy feeling again.

All of the sudden, I started crying. I held out my hand and told my husband, "God told me He's got me. He's got me in the palm of

His hand and He's going to take care of me. He's got me." I was so excited and pumped.

I also had an appointment with Dr. Miller after leaving Dr. Levy's office. It was definitely a busy day.

I still see the joy on her face when we walked into her office and she was able to tell me that all three of the masses had shrunk.

Remember that earlier, she had to tell me that things were not going to get better. Again, I believe that was the textbook version. We knew better. No matter what the books say, we know He is still in the miracle-making business! Our God is the ultimate healer!

Remember the two or three, maybe even nine or ten, things that I guessed I would probably have to go through before being completely healed? I was right. I am still having to fight whatever comes my way. I have learned that some of these fights are not necessarily physical but emotional too. While doing so, I am continuing to hold on to my faith and trust that God has healed me and that He takes care of my emotions. I am so thankful that I have the kind of relationship with Him that I know He will always take care of me. He will never leave me.

Having Him by my side during both physical and emotional challenges has carried me through these difficult times.

When you have a terminal disease, you are fighting for your life. You are fighting every minute of every hour of every day to stay alive. You expect this. You expect the medicines, the doctor visits, and the side effects. You expect the emotions that go along with it. What you do not expect is a phone call like this.

Ring, ring.

It is never good news when you get a phone call at 2:00 in the morning.

"Hello."

"Aunt Dee?"

"Hey, baby."

"My mama is gone."

"What?"

"My mama is gone. We think she had a heart attack," this quiet tiny little voice said over the phone. Totally unexpected. At only sixty-one, my sister, Karen, had passed away. Our niece, Sarah, who had lost her daddy only four and a half years earlier, was calling with this devastating news.

This had to be a nightmare. This could not be real. *Wake up!* It was real. It was no nightmare.

Oh, how I wish I could have held Sarah in my arms that morning. I know her heart was broken.

We had always wished we lived closer instead of in different towns.

We talked a little bit about what happened, and then I asked her if she wanted me to call Granny, my mama, and tell her.

"No. I want to tell her."

So brave. She had been through so much already.

My heart was crushed, and my emotions were all over the place. I loved my sister. She was living life one day, and before we woke up the next morning, she was in heaven.

I could not imagine how my mama was going to feel losing her firstborn. I was going to give Sarah time to call her, then I was going to call her to make sure she was okay, but she called me first. As soon as she hung up from Sarah, she called. My heart broke for her.

I am sure that when she got that kind of phone call, she had thought something had happened to me. I was the one with rare and aggressive terminal cancer. If one of her children was going to pass away, you would have thought it would be me, not my sister.

A heart attack? At sixty-one?

I also have a brother, Timmy. He and Karen were seven and nine years older than me respectively. The two of them always had a special bond because they grew up together and had the same circle of friends. Even though I was the "baby sister," we all loved each other very much.

Karen, Timmy, and Deanna are celebrating
their mama with a Mother's Day lunch.

After my diagnosis, Timmy and I grew very close. We texted almost daily, even if it was just to say, "I love you." We even talked on the phone often, which is rare these days. He lived here in town so we would make it a point to go to lunch or dinner just to spend time together.

Until he pointed it out, I never really thought about it, but my response was "I'm good" every time he asked how I was doing.

"Somebody could punch you in the face and you would get up and say, 'I'm good'!" He rolled his eyes. "Tell me what is really going on."

It became a joke between us.

I slowly started seeing changes in him that we had always prayed for. The way he acted. The things he said. The things he posted on social media.

Shortly after my sister passed away less than a year earlier, he started not feeling well. He kept pushing through as it got worse. It was all happening so quickly.

I had to know. Was he saved? How would he act if I just came out and asked him?

I love God and love to share about what He is doing for me, but I am not pushy about it and I definitely did not want my brother to think I was being pushy. I did not want to push him away.

He had seen how God was working in my life, and we had had several conversations about it.

I finally just came out and asked him one night when we were texting.

"Yes!"

Ah, what a beautiful answer!

He began getting weaker. He ended up moving in with my mama and her husband for them to help him. His daughter, Jessica, would go over before and after work every day to help with him.

His wife had just passed away three years earlier.

He was in and out of the hospital. It broke my heart when I could not go there to be with him. I could not go see him when he was sick at home either because I could not be around anybody with an illness. This went on for months.

Thank God I was able to spend some time with him the last couple of months of his life. I would go to mama's house so we could sit and chat.

Eventually, hospice was called in. This was the first time I ever experienced watching anybody, for lack of a better term, dying. My heart was crushed. I loved my brother so much.

One day I was sitting on the couch with him, just holding his hand and talking to him. He could not really respond. The most he could utter was a slow, "Luh you."

That day, I asked him what I always said to him. Not thinking I would get a response, I was surprised by a very slow, "I'mmm goooddd."

Be still, my heart. Those were the only two words, other than "luh you," that he got out.

The day hospice came out to get him was one of the hardest days of my life. By then, he was not responding at all. As they were rolling him out on the stretcher, I told him I loved him and to remember that "I'm good." I know he heard me. I know he did.

Even though my heart was totally crushed, I could rejoice in the fact that I knew he was going to heaven and that I would see him again one day. I know Jesus was there waiting on him with open arms!

Within a year's time, I had lost both my brother and my sister, both of whom I loved very dearly. As their sister, it was heart-wrenching. Can you even imagine being our mama? Losing two of her babies that close together?

God's love carried us through that very difficult year. Not only did we have to deal with the loss of my brother and sister, we still had to continue to deal with health stuff. Doctor visits, hospital stays, medicines, side effects—you name it, it came our way.

God. God is how we got through it. He gave us strength to get through those very emotional times.

Emotions are also tied into the physical challenges we face on a day-to-day basis. We have learned that we never know what is going to take place from one breath to the next.

Alive. After several opportunities for my life to go in the opposite direction, I am still alive. Still breathing. Still on this earth. There was and is only one answer for this. Only one. That is God. He has kept me here. He has shown me time and time again that He is still in the miracle-making business and that He is the ultimate healer. God.

His love amazes me. I wanted to share it with the world. How could I do this? Where would I start? I wanted people to know what He was doing in my life and that He would do the same for them. How would I get the message out? How could I show my feelings and my love for Him in a way that would honor Him? How could I get others to feel what I was feeling? These thoughts continuously tugged at my heart.

God, what can I do? I want to honor You. I want Your love to shine through. I want people to feel You like I feel You.

Speak to groups—that was what I can do. Okay, so there was my answer, but how would I go about it?

Social media.

Hoping it would work, I put it out there. I posted that I would love to share my story with church groups, community groups, Bible study groups, anybody that would like to have me speak.

It worked! I started getting invitations. I was going to get to share my story! Oh my goodness! I was so excited!

Oh, boy. Now what all would I say? How would I say it? How will I make sure that the people there see God? I did not want the focus to be on me; I wanted it to be on God.

All kinds of thoughts were running through my mind. I had spoken in front of kids for the last thirty years, lots and lots of kids, no biggie, but this will be a room full of adults. This would be different.

My friend is a published author and public speaker who travels all over sharing her message. I contacted her with questions. I researched public speaking, trying to learn everything I could to make it perfect. I was putting a lot of time into the "how" of it.

One afternoon, before my first speaking engagement, Tim and I went to Tybee Island in Georgia. They had the coolest thing ever right on the beach…a swing! Yes, a swing, just like on your front porch. It was awesome!

Deanna is enjoying a fall afternoon swinging at Tybee Island.

With the cool breeze blowing off the ocean and bright sun shining, I sat there for hours, thinking and praying about my upcoming opportunity while he walked up and down the beach looking for shells. It was the perfect fall afternoon.

It hit me like a ton of bricks.

You are not a professional speaker. You are just a girl with a story.

That was it! Why was I trying to make everything so perfect? All that mattered was sharing God's love, sharing what He was doing in my life and what He could do for other people. Speak from my heart. That is all I needed to do.

None of the other stuff mattered.

My first opportunity was at a ladies' circle meeting in a nearby city. It was their Thanksgiving meeting, and you know how those church dinners are when the ladies cook. There were several tables full of good ol' home cooking—turkey, chicken and dumplings, mashed potatoes, sweet potatoes, green beans, corn, macaroni and cheese, and so much more. For dessert? Another table full of pumpkin pie, strawberry shortcake, brownies, cheesecake—mmmmm!

Ronald, a childhood friend of mine, now a preacher at a church close to the one where I was speaking, and his son joined us that evening. In other words, counting Tim, I brought three men to a ladies' circle meeting. Of course they were all welcomed!

All through dinner, even though Tim and I were speaking with everyone around us while we ate, I was going over and over in my mind what I was going to say. I was praying that God would use me for His glory. My main goal was for Him to shine through. I had to remind myself to just "tell my story."

I am not going to lie. I was nervous before I started. I had never done anything like this before. *Please let me remember everything I wanted to say. Please let God shine through and not let it all be about me. Please let it just come from the heart.*

I knew I wanted to share God's love, and that was my chance. I wanted to make Him proud.

I am guessing at the number of people who attended—maybe thirtyish? Praying that hearts would be touched, I noticed that several of the ladies had tears in their eyes as I spoke. That touched me in a way I cannot explain.

It was my first time sharing my story, and God was showing me that He was there with us, that He was touching hearts. It was an amazing feeling, knowing it was not me but that He was using my story to reach others.

After we were finished, a couple of ladies came up to us to share their stories. I remember one lady telling me that it helped her see things differently when I spoke about winning either way—if I was healed on earth, I would win and get to stay with my family; and if Jesus decided to take me to heaven to heal me, I would be a winner too. What was better than being in heaven? I feel like Jesus placed me in that room at that time for that woman to hear what He wanted her to know.

Ronald, my friend I mentioned earlier, invited me to speak on a Sunday morning at his church. Oh wow! A Sunday morning? A church full of people? That would be awesome! *Oh, Jesus, please let me make You proud!*

On that Sunday morning, my mama and her husband came to our house to go with Tim and me. During the forty-five-minute drive to the church, we chitchatted awhile, and then finally I had to say that I needed some quiet time to pray and go over what I would be saying. I did not want to cut off the conversation, but I needed that time to get things straight in my head.

Nancy and Jerry, Deanna's parents, are pausing from their delicious meal to smile for the camera.

When we arrived, I got to see Michelle, Ronald's wife, who was also a childhood friend of mine. The three of us grew up in church together.

As I was speaking, I noticed another childhood friend of mine, Zelda, in the congregation who now lives in that town, as well as Ronald's daddy, who lives in the same hometown as us. They were both visiting that day to show their support.

This was my first time speaking on a Sunday morning. To me, that was huge. At the end of the service, Ronald stepped up and gave his closing remarks. They were beautiful and very heartfelt. He asked people to lift their hands if they would like for him to pray for them.

Several hands went up throughout the congregation as he spoke to them about Jesus welcoming them with open arms, how He would meet their needs, and if they were not certain that He was their Savior, it was a great day to know for sure.

Jesus was working! People were asking Him to come into their hearts! No. It was not me. It was Jesus. *All* Jesus! What a beautiful sight!

After the service, the folks from the congregation had prepared a huge meal with tables full of yummy home-cooked food. While eating, several people came up to us to share their stories. Tim and I both love hearing what God is doing in people's lives.

My first hometown speaking engagement... This will be a Sunday morning I will never forget. Why? Because this was the first time that I had ever spoken in front of that many people I knew.

Deanna is doing one of her favorite things—sharing
the great things God is doing in her life! This is
the first time she spoke in her hometown.

My brother had promised me he would be there, which was a big deal; however, he was too sick to make it. That broke my heart, but I knew he would have been there if he could have. With my sister passing away unexpectedly less than a year earlier and knowing that my brother did not have long to live, my emotions were all over the place.

On the bright side, it was a great day to share about Jesus! As I looked out into the congregation, the pews were about full. Along with the church family was a lot of hometown people I knew. Sitting on the right side of the sanctuary was my mama, her husband, our kids, and our grandbabies filling the first few pews. On the left, there was a huge section of our family from Tim's side and mine—his parents, other in-laws, and cousins—and throughout the congregation were groups of our friends. It was awesome to see their support.

Looking out over the congregation, I could see people's raw emotions. Knowing that God was working through me to help others was an incredible feeling. It was not about me but about Him and what He could and would do for everyone if they would just accept Him into their hearts and build a relationship with Him.

The altar call at the end of the service was absolutely beautiful. People came to the front to kneel at the altar, giving their heart to Jesus and praying for others. My heart was overjoyed!

When it was over, they asked Tim and me to stand at the back of the church to speak to people as they were leaving.

The lady who told us she was a visitor that day came through the line and told me that she had a gift for me. She told us that she had battled cancer. She handed me a ring and said that she wore it when times got tough. She said that she would rub it to remind her that God was taking care of her and that she could make it through whatever she was facing. The ring, which fit me perfectly, had a second layer on it that would actually spin around; it read "I can do all things through Christ who strengthens me."

Wow! What a special gift...and from somebody we did not even know! To add to that, nobody seemed to know her.

I remember seeing the lady sitting all alone on the front row. A friend of mine who goes to that church asked around, and nobody knew her. Eventually, days later, we found out that she was a friend to someone who was involved in the service.

It was like she was an angel sent there to help me stay positive during difficult times.

Every time I have had the opportunity to speak has been special. Something always happens to make the time memorable.

I received a prayer blanket crocheted with loving hands when I spoke at another hometown church. A girl whom I have known since elementary school invited me to speak at their ladies' meal. More loving ladies. More great food. Better yet? More great stories of what God has done and is doing in people's lives.

One thing about sharing my story to this group and other groups is that I see the reactions on people's faces. I see the love glowing in their eyes and the tears rolling down their faces. Most importantly, I feel the presence of God in the room.

When I finished sharing my story at this meeting, my friend blessed me with the blanket she had crocheted. I remember her telling me how she prayed over the blanket for me.

I added this blanket to the collection of ones I have that people have given me since I was first diagnosed. I love, love, love my prayer blankets. Tim and I have put them in order on the blanket ladder he built me so that each time I go for a chemo treatment, I take a different one and lay it over me while I am receiving the medication. This way, I am always covered in prayers while I am there.

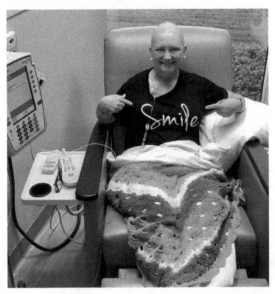

There is always something to smile about! The handmade crocheted prayer blanket that Deanna received as a gift is a reminder to her that she is covered in prayers as she is getting her treatment.

While speaking at a church in a neighboring town, we witnessed a beautiful sight. It was another ladies' dinner, and the fellowship building was full of church members and their guests. The lights were low, and beautiful decorations were all around.

Even though that was all beautiful in itself, that was not the beautiful sight we witnessed.

When I finished speaking, the preacher's wife also spoke. In the closing prayer, they asked people to raise their hands if they wanted to give their lives to Jesus or know more about Him.

Of course our eyes were closed at the time, but after the prayer, you could see little groups of people all around praying, crying, and giving their hearts to Jesus. Saying it was incredible is an understatement. Right there in that room, people's lives were changing for the better, changing forever. It was a beautiful sight!

One afternoon, I had an engagement scheduled and I was not feeling well at all. Not at all. There was no way I was going to cancel it. I prayed that Jesus would help me get through it and help me to show His love while I was speaking.

Tim and I got to speak to a few ladies with beautiful stories while we were eating. It always makes me so happy to hear all the wonderful things that God is doing in people's lives.

Before I spoke, I did need a short break. I went into the kitchen to be by myself for a few minutes. I say by myself, but of course Tim was with me, and my cousin, Leigh Anne, who is a nurse, also went in there with us. We were not in there that long—just till I got myself feeling a little better so I could go back out and share my story.

The time had come. Dinner was finished, and it was time for me to speak. *God, please help me. Please give me energy to be uplifting while sharing Your story.* He answered my prayers. I was able to do what I felt like He would have me do—and that was to share His love.

When I finished speaking, we did not hang around and talk to people like we normally did. I told my friend who invited me that I felt awful and needed to go home. She understood, but it hurt my heart. I enjoy talking to the folks afterward.

It did not take long for us to find out what was wrong. I guess the "not feeling so well" was all leading up to this.

"Deanna? Deanna?" my husband called as he walked into the bedroom and saw the blank look on my face. I was sitting on the bed. He said I had slowly turned my head to look at him. He started to ask me questions.

"Are you okay? What day is it?"

He said I slowly got the answers out. He knew something was not right and immediately took me to the hospital.

When we arrived, they took me straight back into triage and began running tests. I was admitted, and the tests continued.

Again? A double? This time, I had not only had a stroke; I had a double stroke—one on each side of my brain. I did not even know you could have two strokes at once. I never actually thought about it, but now that it was happening, I never knew it could.

Here we go again. Doctors, nurses, every therapist you can think of, coming in and out of my room, doing test after test after test after test. Could I walk straight? Could I walk by myself? Could I brush my teeth? Could I get in and out of the bed by myself? Could I swallow apple sauce? Could I swallow graham crackers? Could I swallow water? Could I drink through a straw? Could I speak clearly?

It seemed that when things were all said and done, there was no residual—just like from the first stroke.

Only a couple of months later, the same thing happened again. "Deanna? Talk to me."

He said I had slowly turned my head and looked at him.

"What day is it? What are you watching?"

He said that I had the exact same symptoms as I had when they had diagnosed me with the double stroke. I answered his questions, but very slowly.

We immediately went to the hospital. Just like before, the tests started immediately. I was admitted, like I was every time. Therapists started coming in to work with me. Only this time, we had different results.

The doctor on call told us that the tests were not showing a stroke; it sounded like I had a mini stroke. Mini strokes are different from strokes. They dissolve on their own and do not leave permanent damage.

Even though any kind of stroke is scary to deal with, at least we know this one did not leave any residual for sure.

Ah, you know…just hanging out at the hospital with
Wende, Jeremy, Alisha, Kim, Tim, and Mama. Deanna's
friends and family show her strong support.

Cancer causes a person's blood to thicken, which can cause it to clot, which can cause a stroke. Of course this was why we had to take blood thinners.

A cancer patient's life involves many vicious cycles. One thing leads to another to another to another. A stroke is just one example.

Another example is what it does to your teeth. During my last visit to the dentist, I could not help it. The tears began to trickle down my cheeks even though I was trying hard to hold them back. I am not the kind of person to let my emotions go in public, but this time I could not help myself.

Our niece, Meagan, is my dental assistant. She and I were the only ones in the room after the dentist had finished checking my teeth and speaking with me. This routine visit, unfortunately, led to a lot more than X-rays and a cleaning.

I know. It is silly for a fifty-five-year-old lady to cry when she is at the dentist. Considering my teeth have never been that great to begin with, I have had plenty of work done over the years. Never have I cried when I was told what needed to be done.

This time was different. The chemo had taken its toll even more. My teeth were decaying worse. I was starting to have trouble with my gums. I had a couple of cavities. Meagan even shared information with me about a partial to replace the teeth I had already lost.

As she was explaining my options, the tears started.

"This is not your fault, Aunt Dee. Aunt Dee, this is not your fault."

She said this to me several times as she tried to comfort me. I felt bad for breaking down in front of her. I knew it was not my fault—it was just something else I had to deal with. I explained this to her.

All I could think of is I have a trach to help me breathe. Now I am going to have a partial to help me chew, and I have been told by the doctor that I need hearing aids because I do not hear well. Looking for the positive in the situation, I had Lasik many years ago so I do not have to wear contacts anymore although I do wear readers. Plus another good thing is I have hair now, so at least I am not bald anymore.

I am not going to lie. It is very hard having to depend on so many things to help me with everyday life. When I start feeling down about it, I have to remind myself that these are all blessings that are keeping me active and giving me a better quality of life. I feel like I am too young to have these things happening already. I know. I am not that young, but inside, I feel a lot younger than I am.

So the tears at the dentist? Stress. Not necessarily because I had to have dental work done but because it was just more things I would have to deal with. I was thinking of all the "extras" I had to have from the neck up to keep me going.

Growing up, my mama taught me that pretty is as pretty does and that what is on the inside is what counts. I am glad she did because my, how looks can change. We all change as we get older, but I, as that cute little college cheerleader back in the day, never dreamed I would be rocking a bald head while having a trach, a partial, and hearing aids! As far as the inside goes, I feel beautiful now and I am grateful to my mama for that.

Time to switch gears. Now, think about this: a juicy rib eye steak; a delicious baked potato soaked with butter, sour cream, and a few dashes of salt and pepper; and a beautiful green salad with all the fixings! Yep! The perfect meal. The perfect meal with great company—my son, daughter, friend, and her mom. We went to a restaurant here in town that we had not been to in years. The food was delicious, and we enjoyed our time together laughing at stories and having just good ol' plain conversation.

About thirty minutes after getting home, I was sitting on the love seat watching TV with Tim. Ouch! That felt sort of like an ant bite. I felt a strange little pain on the inside of my upper right arm. I reached over to see if maybe there was an ant or something. I did not feel anything. There were no bites. A few minutes later, ouch! It happened several times and started in the same place on the inside of my upper left arm.

I went to the bathroom to pull off my shirt so I could look in the mirror and see what was going on. On both arms were big red welts and, man, were they itching! The welts started spreading down the front of my body—a few spots here, a few spots there. I thought it was kind of weird that they were just on the front and not the back. They spread all the way to my feet. I took an antihistamine to see if that would help. Ohhh, they were itching so bad. Tim kept telling me to quit scratching. Really? That was a lot easier said than done, but I did honestly try not to. What else could I do, and what was causing them? I decided to take a bath in Epsom salt, which I later learned was not the best idea.

Oh my goodness. After getting out of the tub, I was so weak and felt so bad that I literally sprawled out face-down across the bed—butt naked—with just my towel. I did not even take time to dry off or put clothes on. I remember feeling miserable. The rash was a lot worse, with big red welts all over the front of my body. I looked like a cheetah with red spots.

Within just a few short minutes, I had to go to the bathroom.

Here is where it really started getting bad. As soon as I sat down, I could tell I was fixing to pass out. I called for Tim. He came in at the perfect time and caught me as I was falling forward. I had no idea of what was happening. I could hear him talking to me, but I could not answer. He said my eyes rolled back in my head while it was coming out both ends.

I remember hearing him call my name over and over, "Deanna! Deanna!" He was taking care of me and calling 911 at the same time. Feeling scared and helpless, he thought he was losing me. He was worried.

Thinking back, I remember hearing him talk to the dispatcher, but I could not tell what he was saying. All I could hear was mumbling.

Thank God he was able to get me awake, cleaned up, and dressed before the firefighters and EMTs arrived. Bless his heart, he also got the bathroom cleaned up while keeping a steady check on me.

Even though I was still groggy, I do remember the loud sounds of the sirens as they were approaching our house. It seemed like our living room was full of emergency workers asking all kinds of questions.

It was not long before they put me on a gurney and loaded me into the ambulance. Tim was in his truck, ready to follow us to the hospital.

We were on our street in the ambulance for a while, lights still flashing brightly. In fact, Tim came out there to check on me to make sure everything was all right. We learned that night that the emergency workers have to do several things on-site in the ambulance before they leave for the hospital. That was why it was taking so long.

On the way to the hospital, I remember the paramedic asking me if I was going to throw up. He offered me this funky-looking blue bag in case I needed to.

"No, I'm fine."

That changed within seconds.

"Give me the bag. Quick! I'm going to be sick."

Thank goodness he was able to get me the bag in time! How in the world do paramedics not puke when they smell or see their patients throwing up?

Anyway, by the time we got to the hospital, the welts were even worse. Other than giving me fluids, I do not remember what else they did to clear them up. Oh, they definitely did more, I just do not remember what they gave me.

As I am writing this and reliving that night, I am reminded how great God is and how He not only kept me safe but stuck right by Tim's side every step of the way. Clearly, his hands were full keeping me alive, calling 911, cleaning up after me, explaining to the emergency workers what was happening, and getting to the hospital to be with me. Our God is amazing. He never ever leaves our side.

Wende, my friend who went out to eat with us that night, came to visit me in the hospital. I looked terrible. She was as surprised as we were at how bad the welts were.

While she was there, a lady came in and offered to rub my feet to help me feel better. Of course I took her up on it. There would have been no question about that! Wende, being the good friend that she is—and only a good friend would offer to do this—said, "Well, if that makes her feel better, I'll rub her feet." And she did.

Within a few short minutes, the rash spread to my bald head. Yep! All over my head were big red welts. Tim and I started kidding her, saying that I was allergic to her; I had been with her at the restaurant the night I broke out, and then the rash spread to my head after she rubbed my feet. It became a joke that she was causing the rash.

To this day, we have no idea what caused all of that to happen. My oncologist said it was not the chemo because too many days had passed since my last treatment. The allergist they sent me to said it was not the food I ate because it would have happened within minutes after eating it.

He ran allergy tests on me to try to find an answer. The test showed that I was allergic to—are you ready for this?—dust mites and cedar trees. Well, there is dust everywhere, and we are outdoor people—I have been all my life—so I am used to being around cedar trees. Obviously, neither of those gave us answers to the current scare.

The allergist prescribed an EpiPen for me just in case and wrote instructions for a test a doctor would administer if it ever happens again. Not knowing the cause, we had no idea whether it would reoccur.

Probably a year and a half, or two years later, we were having a girls' weekend at the beach. Denise, another one of my sisterfriends, and I went down earlier than everyone else. It was March, so being the big sports fan that she was, she was trying to figure out how to get the TV in the condo to work so she could watch March Madness—especially the big rivalry game between Carolina and Duke coming on that night. Determined to get the TV on, she realized after about forty-five minutes that there was a switch on the wall that turned on the power.

While she was working on the TV, I started feeling those little "bites" again. This time, they started on my legs. Oh, man, were they itching! They started to spread. I showed them to her and told her that was what happened the last time. She saw firsthand how they just appeared out of nowhere. They just start popping up.

I called my oncology nurse. I explained what was going on and that I had taken two antihistamines. She talked to my oncologist, and because of what happened the first time, she told us to go to the emergency room.

Oh, no—not during March Madness! Of course, Denise told me we were not worrying about the games; we were getting to the hospital. To her surprise, they had the tournament on in the waiting room when we got there. Perfect.

This was a small case, and we wanted to keep it that way. Because I had taken the medicine and a good bit of time had lapsed, the welts were gone by the time the doctor came into the room. In other words, an ER visit at the beach that cost me over five hundred dollars with nothing to show the doctor, was a good thing since the welts cleared up, but who wants to spend that kind of money at the hospital or even go to the hospital during a girls' weekend?

What was causing this to happen? That was twice now that it had. We still had no answers.

Oh, did I mention that when the rest of our friends arrived at the condo and called to see where we were, Denise told them not to mess with the switch on the wall because she had everything set for the games? Even though it became a joke, she was actually serious.

You know how there is always that one friend. Well, as that one friend came in, she was hunting for the light switch, and what did she do? Yep! She turned off the switch on the wall that controlled the TV! Luckily, she had everything working when we got back; however, we ended up watching the big game on a screen the size of the wall at the restaurant we went to that night. That was better than watching it on TV anyway!

Maybe another year had passed; I'm not sure, but it was a good while. I woke up with my legs itching, and there they were again—welts. Ugly red welts. You have got to be kidding me! What is causing these crazy things to pop up randomly? There were not a lot, but they were there on both thighs.

While I was in the shower, they spread down my legs. That "not a lot there" quickly changed to a whole lot—all over my legs. Some of them were huge, as if multiple ones had merged together. My legs looked awful.

Tim brought me two antihistamines, hoping that would take care of it.

Knowing that we would be leaving the following day to go to the mountains for a week, I contacted Dr. Levy. We put a plan into place. Thank goodness the medicine did the trick again, so we did not have to worry about it—for several days anyway. Yeah…several days without the welts, then they decided to make another appearance.

While in the mountains, I woke up itching. Oh, no, here we go again. Sure enough, there they were. Big, red, ugly welts. Another rash. We followed through with my doctor's plan—thank goodness we had one in place—and everything was fine.

Remember my friend, Wende, whom we kidded about me being allergic to? The one whom we told caused me to break out? She visited us in the mountains on that trip.

"See? I'm allergic to you! You came to see me, and I broke out!"

She knew we were kidding. It was all in fun, or was it? Nah, she knew we were playing.

It was obviously some kind of allergic reaction, but to what? What kept causing it? I cannot help but think there was something in my body causing it to happen. It was wild how so much time had lapsed in between each episode. There were no common factors. It just happened. We just pray it is never again as severe as it was that first time.

Considering we have yet to discover what has caused the rashes and welts to break out on my body, we do know it is not the chemo; however, the chemo has caused many other side effects over the years that has made me feel like I am on a roller coaster.

To give you an idea of how severe the conditions can be, I am fixing to take you on a side-effect ride. Hang on!

Here we go! Up, up, up…almost at the top…swerve to the left…staying high…spiraling down, round and round and round. Back to the bottom. Here we go again…up, up, up—with a little shaking—check out this hill… Down we go. Aaaah! Look! A big curve! Hang on! Sharply jerked to the left, then back to the right… climbing, climbing, climbing…this hill is enormous…Aaaaaaah! Oh my goodness…*look!* A huge upside-down loop! *Aaaaaaah!* Ah… finally…a straight track. I can catch my breath.

This, my friends, is the perfect explanation of the life of a cancer patient. One minute you are on top of the world. Everything is going fine. Things start to change. Then you are spiraling down, not understanding what is happening to your body. Side effects start to set in. Your body is doing things you never thought of. The next thing you know, you are on your way back up again. This round of side effects is starting to heal, and you feel much better. You are thrown another curve, then another—jerked this way, then that way. More side effects. Finally, you are back on top of the world, and things are going great. Life is good. Swoosh! Downhill you go, your life turned upside down, and before you know it, you are back right side up and starting over again.

Knowing this is how things are, how could anyone go through this crazy journey without God? Through every single bump, no matter how small or how large, He carries me. Through every hill I climb, every obstacle I face, He is there. I have no doubts.

My faith in God, staying positive, and the incredible support I have on my side are the three main things that keep me sane through the multitude of challenges I have to face each day.

Every time a new side effect decides to show its ugly self, we call it a bump in the road, and with Tim's help we work through it. We do not really talk much about the bumps; he just jumps right in and does whatever needs to be done—applies the medicine and bandages, rubs my back and wipes my face when I have been sick, rubs my feet when the neuropathy is bothering me—he takes care of the problem and never complains a bit.

It was not until one evening when he and I went to dinner with a friend we had not seen in a long while that I was amazed at what we had been through. It was a different kind of amazement.

Our friend wanted to know about the side effects, so we began to tell him. That night, hearing us actually say out loud what we had experienced to that point, was an incredible eye-opener. Looking back, I guess I had pushed a lot of them out of my memory so I would not focus on them. Man, we had made it through a lot! The side effects had been horrific!

I knew there were bad ones. I knew we had dealt with a lot, but I did my best to remain positive while they were happening and focused on getting well. I reckon this is why the severity of them was not sticking with me.

Was I always positive? Oh no, I definitely had my share of breaking down and crying. I just always told myself it could be worse.

Riding home from dinner that night, Tim and I discussed all the insane conditions we had shared with our friend. We were both feeling the misery each situation brought. Before I get into some of these, I want to point out that some of them will fall into that "too much information" category and you may want to skip over them. I am not trying to gross you out; however, my life has been full of the good, the bad, and the ugly. If I am to share my story, it is all part of it.

The boatload of various chemotherapies I have been on have caused different side effects. It has been over four years since I have been getting treatments, and to be honest, I can only remember the ones that matched up with the first round of treatments. After that, it has all been a blur. The medicines and side effects all run together, and I have no idea what side effect went with what treatment. I remember the side effects; I just do not remember the chemotherapy they went with. Like I mentioned earlier, I pushed my way through them and kept on kicking!

Here we are, over four years later, still fighting side effects that have been a lot more severe than they were the first go-round.

I will start at the point in which I could not remember what caused what. That is okay, though, considering it does not really matter. Remember? Everybody is different and is affected in different ways.

One morning, I woke up to see blood on my pillow and dried blood on my face. Instead of my nose just running pure liquid because of a lack of nose hairs, it decided it was also going to bleed. Out of nowhere came the blood. Not a bad side effect, but an inconvenient one. I never knew when or where it was going to happen or how long it would last. We could count on it happening multiple times a day.

Have you ever thought about how much you use your elbows or how hard they are to heal? More than likely not, because really, who would think about something like that? Why would anybody think about that? We noticed that the skin on my elbows started to crack. Not badly at first, but as time went on, the skin on them started to become very thin and crack a lot more.

Once again, I woke up one morning with blood in my bed. This time it was on the sheets and on my pillow. What in the world? During the night, my elbows had started bleeding.

In the beginning, several Band-Aids on each elbow took care of it. Each time Tim changed the bandages, he was so gentle. He took his time so that he would not hurt me. One day, I got the bright idea to change them myself. Well, instead of being gentle, I just ripped off the first one. *Dumb mistake!* Because my skin had become so thin, I literally ripped through layers of it. I could actually see the layers! Talking about hurting! Oh my goodness, my arm hurt for days! It burned like crazy! Believe me, that was the last time I messed with changing anything on my elbows!

Think about how many times you bend your elbows a day, how many times you use them to push yourself out of bed or a chair, how many times you push open a door, or anything else you do with them. With all that action, the Band-Aids we started with did not work for long. Elbows do not heal easily but they do get worse quickly, especially when someone like me rips through the layers of skin.

Before long, Tim had to start wrapping both of my arms from the top to the bottom because the sores were getting worse, growing bigger, and bleeding more. For them to heal, I had to look like a mummy. For several weeks, he would wrap them twice a day, every morning and every night.

As I write this, I see just how much we have woken up to during the years. I always say we never know what is going to happen from one minute to the next, and by writing about when a lot of these side effects started, I am realizing we have no idea what we will wake up to the next morning either.

For example, there was a period of time that I dreaded opening my mouth when I woke up. Who, me? The person who talks all the time? Day and night? Even in my sleep? I knew that once I did… oh…it would hurt so bad. You see, one of the chemotherapies gave me severe—and I mean severe—dry mouth.

Imagine your tongue being superglued to the roof of your mouth. Now try to pull it off. Imagine the pain and agony of doing so. Yeah, that is how it felt. As I pulled it down, it literally felt like I was pulling off layers of skin from it. This was one of the most painful side effects I have had to deal with. Every morning, I would cry because it hurt so bad. Yes, I used the magic mouthwash—tons of it. Yes, I used the over-the-counter sprays. Yes, they helped in the moment, but that was it. I am not complaining because at least they helped then. It was just the mornings when I had to pull my tongue down that were so excruciating.

Along with the awful pain of my tongue being "superglued" to the roof of my mouth, the inside of my mouth was covered in white sores. They hurt so incredibly bad that it was hard for us to find things that I could eat. The foods had to be soft, like creamed potatoes or macaroni and cheese; or liquid, like soups. Anything spicy would hurt, so there was none of that.

What is that? What is what? Oh yeah, the infamous chemo brain that you have all probably heard about. It is real. Trust me. Sometimes it causes me to get my words mixed up when I speak or forget what I am trying to say. I have to really think about what is coming out of my mouth. Thankfully, this does not happen a lot. I cannot help but wonder if it is all chemo brain or if the multiple strokes had something to do with my having to put extra effort into what I am saying at times.

I mentioned fatigue in my first round of side effects. The fact is, fatigue is a huge side effect with most chemo drugs; at least it has been with my experience. At times, weakness comes along with it. My hands have actually felt so weak that Tim had to open bottles for me. Not only can chemotherapy drugs cause a person to be tired and weak, so can anemia. Yep, you got it. At one point, I was anemic. When this happens, your red blood cell count is low.

"You need a blood transfusion."

What? A blood transfusion? How do I know that's safe? How do I know that I will not get bad blood from somebody who sold their plasma?

I was assured that it is perfectly safe and that it goes through many screenings before it is ever given to patients.

After the transfusion, I immediately felt better. I was so thankful and surprised at how quickly I felt like myself again.

You have already read about the horrible experience I had losing my hair during my first round of chemotherapy. Well, it happened again once I started back on the treatments. I had to go through it all again. Just like the first time, it was miserable. I cried and cried and then cried some more. I kept telling myself that it will grow back to stop crying so much but it was hard. That was when I had to keep reminding myself that it may have been hard but I could do hard things. I actually remind myself of that a lot.

There was one major difference this time. Wende did not shave it off. We went to her shop, but this time, instead of her being the one to cut it off, Tim did. Yes—my husband cut it and then shaved off what was left. We did not know he had barber skills! I have decided if it ever happens again—I hope it does not, but if it does—I want our four grandbabies to do the cutting. There is no telling how it would turn out, but that would not matter considering it all has to be shaved off in the end. I am sure that is something they would never forget!

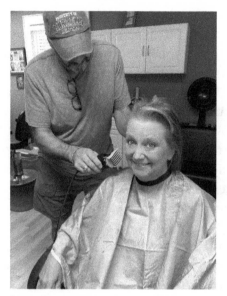

There it is! After many tears have been shed over losing her hair, Deanna finally shares a smile once Tim begins shaving her head.

Have you ever seen a monkey pick bugs out of another monkey's hair and eat them? That is what we looked like. No kidding, except Tim definitely did not eat what he found, and no, I did not have bugs in my hair. However, I did have bumps and sores. After my hair had grown back the first time, I started getting little itchy bumps on my head, of all things. They multiplied quickly and turned into bigger bumps that turned into sores on my head, about thirty of them. I know, that sounds really gross. You are right. It was. The good thing was that my hair had grown back by then and covered them up. Can you imagine a bald head with about thirty sores all over it? Now that is just nasty.

Once again, my gracious husband to the rescue. Now picture this. He would dig through my hair and put ointment on each sore every day. We would laugh about it because we would say he looked like the monkeys do when they look for bugs on other monkeys to eat.

Speaking of nasty... At my age I have to put on what? I am going to have to wear what? An adult diaper? At fifty-one? I should not have had to wear an adult diaper, but I did not have a choice. Well, I reckon I did, but if I had chosen not to wear one, we would have been cleaning up messes constantly.

Boy, I feel funny writing about this, but then again, it is part of it. While taking a pill twice a day at home for chemo instead of going to the hospital for infusions, I found out at lightning speed that chemo diarrhea is no joke. Having very little control over what seemed like straight water pouring out of me multiple times a day, I did not have a choice but to wear the diapers. It had a mind of its own, came when it wanted, even in the middle of the night. It was not choosy.

There was an upside to this nastiness. I lost close to forty pounds because of it. Do not get me wrong. I was super glad about getting rid of the weight, but that was *not* the way I wanted to lose it.

And, oh, did I mention these pills cost $15,000–$20,000 a month? Insurance refused to pay for them, but thank God a foundation backed me and paid for them in full. That was definitely a godsend in itself! Needing a particular drug to help keep you alive but knowing the insurance company is keeping you from getting it is not a good feeling whatsoever. In my opinion? It is flat-out wrong. My doctors know what is best for me, not the insurance company.

When I say we never know what is going to happen from one minute to the next, this proves it. I mean really, a snake? Out of my foot?

"What are you doing?"

"Pulling a snake out of my foot."

"What?"

"Pulling a snake out of my foot. I just pulled a little stick out before this."

"Deanna, wake up. You're dreaming."

I sure was. I had been having a lot of crazy dreams lately. It had to be the new meds. Along with new immunotherapy drug came the off-the-wall dreams.

In this particular one, there was what looked like a tiny zit on the bottom of my foot. Something poked through the top of it as I began squishing it. I squeezed a little harder. A very thin stick started coming out of my foot. You read that right. A stick! It was small, but yes, it was a stick. It even had a leaf on it. I know, crazy, right? There was another zit, this one a little larger. As I started to pinch it, something small and white popped through. It looked like—oh my goodness, it was a worm! I grabbed it between my thumb and pointer finger and started pulling. It kept coming and coming and getting bigger and bigger. It was not a worm at all. It was a snake! Oooh, gross! Unknowingly to me, because I was still asleep, I was sitting straight up in bed with my fingers pinched, pulling a snake from my foot.

Another night, I elbowed Tim, waking him up. He said that I was jerking all around.

"Deanna, wake up!"

"They're holding me hostage!"

I was fighting in my dream and undoubtedly in bed too, considering I had just elbowed my husband. I would have never done that if I had been awake.

Who knew that one of the side effects would be having crazy, and I mean crazy, dreams?

Speaking of crazy… I do not consider this a side effect, but it is odd, so I am adding it here after a couple of my crazy dream descriptions. For whatever reason, I craved pickles. Pickles? Yes, pickles. In the beginning, I only wanted the ones from Clawson's. For months, I ate them day and night. After a while, the craving changed to bread and butter pickles. Why? I have seriously never in my life wanted bread and butter pickles, but for some strange reason, that is the kind I started to crave. A little later on, the craving turned to dill. I am telling you the truth when I say I could sit and eat a *whole jar* of pickles—not one, not two, but the *whole jar*!

One night, Brett and I had a waitress whose mother had ovarian cancer. Without us mentioning pickles whatsoever, she told us that her mother craved them all the time. Undoubtedly, there was something to the pickle craving!

I have learned so much through this journey. There is one thing in particular that I should have done differently.

If you are ever in this same situation, make sure you tell your oncologist when your body is feeling different in any kind of way. I did not, and it caused things to get worse.

Neuropathy decided to move in on my feet and fingers. Dr. Miller and my oncology nurses would ask me about it at every visit. My answer was always the same: "It's no biggie. I only feel it every now and then." Even though I was noticing it more and more, in my mind, it would go away if I did not focus on it. Wrong answer.

Imagine having washcloths wrapped thickly around your feet, with duct tape wrapped around that. That is how my feet felt. I had no control over my toes anymore. I could not spread them no matter how hard I tried, nor could I pick things up with them. I know. I know. That sounds weird, but yes, I used to pick up things with my toes. That would drive Tim crazy, but I had done it since I was a little girl, so it was normal to me.

My feet would get so cold that I felt like they were frostbitten. It felt like I could thump them, and they would literally fall off. When they got like this, I also felt like I walked funny.

The tingling in my fingers gradually grew stronger—never horrible, but stronger. This caused me to hit the wrong letters on the keyboard by not being able to feel where my fingers were placed. Worse yet, it caused me to drop things. Sometimes whatever I was holding would just fall out of my hand. Luckily, it would come and go.

If I had not ignored the neuropathy, it may not have gotten as bad as it did. Dr. Miller could have helped control it. I did not realize the severity of it at the time.

Along this journey, I had to deal with the red devil, a harsh chemotherapy. This next situation is what I had to do to try to fight off the side effects for this particular drug.

When it was administered, I had to sit on ice. Not actually sit on ice—my fanny was not on ice—but about everything else was. Both my feet and hands were put in plastic bags, and then I had to keep them on ice in tubs throughout the infusion. Also, I had to eat ice chips throughout the whole treatment. If I did not do these things, the chemo would burn my hands, feet, and the inside of my mouth. This never got easy, but I grew more used to it as time went on.

Most of the chemotherapy drugs that have been given to me lasted for months at a time. We would deal with the side effects of each one till they got so bad that Dr. Miller would stop that drug and start another one after a healing break.

Deciding to take a different route, we changed to immunotherapy. After the first treatment, I did not feel any side effects. It was great! I was hoping this was the way it would be the whole time.

After the second? Whew! My, how life changed. Fatigue was major. Some weakness set in. I began feeling sad more often. My appetite decreased, yet I had gained close to ten pounds. I was not as stable on my feet. Looking in the mirror, I did not recognize the person looking back at me. All I saw was some woman with a big, puffed-up face with huge bags under her squinty eyes.

Wanting to get outside for a little bit, Tim set up the hammock for me so I could enjoy the fresh, cool breeze blowing through the trees. While lying there, tears started to stream down my face.

"Are you okay?"

"I'm just having a moment."

He reached over and rubbed my hand, then went inside.

What is wrong with me? I feel awful. Am I dying and do not know it?

All kinds of thoughts were running through my head about the way I was feeling. Hopefully, I could get an answer at my appointment the following day at the lab.

Because of the COVID scare, all cancer patients are tested for the virus a couple of days before their treatment. Even though I was not scheduled to see Dr. Miller on the day of my virus testing, I was hoping to get some kind of answer. When the nurses saw my face, they both agreed that I needed to see her. Luckily, we were able to grab her on her way to surgery to look at me.

"You look like a cupcake."

"I like that better than a blowfish. That's what I've been saying I look like. Tim still tells me I'm beautiful, but I believe he's telling me a story."

"It's the truth. Less wrinkles this way!"

Now you know one of the many reasons I love Dr. Miller. She makes me smile. She has a way about her. She is straight to the point when she needs to be, which is sometimes hard to take, but we love her honesty and appreciate knowing what we have to deal with up front. Along with that, she is funny and makes us laugh. She makes us feel comfortable and at peace. My whole family believes in her wholeheartedly, and we know that I am safe in her hands.

Because she was on her way to surgery, she told me she would let me know about my face. Following through as always, she called me the next day.

"Hello. I know why your face looks like it does. Your thyroid isn't functioning properly. You have severe hypothyroidism. This is a side effect of the immunotherapy drug."

"What do we do?"

"I'm prescribing you medication to start taking today. Then take one pill each day after that. We will make an appointment for you to see an endocrinologist."

I was not thrilled about adding my thyroid to the list of what we have to deal with; neither was I happy about taking more medicine. But considering the symptoms were not of the cancer spreading, I was glad to hear it. I was not dying. It was just another bump in the road. It could be controlled.

While I had her on the phone, I asked her about the results of the CT scan I had earlier in the week. Waiting for the results is always so hard.

Oh, thank God! Music to my ears! One mass had shrunk and the other two had grown just a tiny bit. That was super, considering, for different reasons, I had not had but two treatments in five months. And the COVID test I mentioned above? Negative. All in all, a good day of reports.

With all of the side effects mentioned above, plus others like headaches, leg cramps, losing my balance, easy bruising, constipation, and more, I sometimes wondered if they were also due to the strokes and now from the hypothyroidism?

Ya know? My body has to wonder what in the world is going on considering all the hits it has taken over the past several years.

The one thing I do know is that everybody needs them a Tim in their life. Only an honorable man like him would stick by his woman through all of the struggles that cancer brings, and just thinking, the side effects are only a small part of the day-to-day living of a patient with a terminal disease that their caretaker is involved in.

This man right here, Tim, really knows
how to make Deanna smile!

Having said this, caretakers deserve much more credit than they get. I am not talking about getting money or actual public recognition. I am thinking more on the lines of people checking on them. I am very thankful for the support our family gets. We are blessed, but I think a lot about Tim. Do people check in on him? Do they ever ask him how he feels? Do they ask if he needs anything? Does he have somebody who he breaks down in front of? Because I never see it. He stays strong in front of me to keep me strong. I know he gets scared. I am sure there are times he has no idea what to say or do, but I would never know it. Fighting these struggles for over four years is a long time for him to stick by my side day in and day out.

Deanna thinks everybody needs them a Tim! Here the two lovebirds are spending a fall afternoon posing for a photoshoot. Photo Credit: Crystal Pearson Photography

Not only has this amazing husband of mine fought through the side effects with me, he has been with me every single step of the way. He has been to every doctor visit, every test, every scan, every speaking engagement, every appointment, every treatment, and has even spent every night in the hospital with me, up until COVID restrictions were put into place.

However, Tim being Tim, COVID restrictions or not, he still found a way to be with me or close to me most of the time. He still drove me to every appointment and sat in his truck in the parking deck after he dropped me off at the front door of the facility. During an appointment for an upcoming hernia surgery, we included him on speakerphone while my surgeon explained what was going on and what the plans were for the surgery. We did this on several different doctor visits. This way, he was a part of the conversation, and to be honest, another set of ears to help me remember what the doctors said. It is easy for me to get overwhelmed with all the information being thrown our way, but thankfully, he remembers.

He was not able to be stay with me at the hospital for my hernia surgery, but they did let him sit in the waiting room, with instructions of course. Are you ready for this? These were the actual words, close enough anyway, of the lady who called me ahead of time.

"You may have one visitor. They may come into the waiting room and have a seat. They may stay the entire time and speak to the surgeon afterward, or they can leave and someone will call them to keep them updated on your surgery. If they choose to stay, they may only get up to go to the restroom. They cannot wander the halls. If they leave, they may not return."

I added this in here because I thought it was pretty funny that they were giving grown adults permission to go to the restroom.

Of course he stayed until he could speak with my surgeon so he would know that things went well and that I was okay. This was my first hospital stay without him, so for five very long days, we spoke on the phone multiple times a day instead of in person. I missed him being there greatly.

During this hospital stay, I did have one visitor for a few short minutes. No, he did not come into the hospital; that was not allowed. However, I did receive a text that told me to look outside my window. There stood our son, Brett. He was holding a sign that he made. It read "Get Well Mom Love You!" Awwww! What a great way to brighten my day! He definitely brought some happiness to this mama.

Brett is not letting hospital restrictions stop him from letting
his mama know he loves her while she is in the hospital.

Remember how I told you earlier that Tim finds ways to be
near me even with COVID restrictions in place? Well, on the days I
have infusions, you will find him sitting in his lounge chair outside
the hospital window of the cubby where I am having my treatment.
With only the tinted window between us, reading his book, there he
sits, no matter the weather. The oncology nurses all think he is great!
They make sure that I always get a cubby with a window so he can
be with me.

Even if he has to sit outside her window, Tim is always by
Deanna's side while she is getting her chemo treatment.

One day when I had an appointment, I asked him if he wanted to take a break and not go.

"Are you taking a break?" he asked me.

"No."

"Well, I am not taking a break either."

He is constantly checking on me to make sure I am okay and have what I need (and want). He even does the cooking and the washing. He is definitely, in my opinion, a multiple-time winner of the Husband of the Year Award!

His love for me makes me think of God's love for us all. He will never leave us. He is always by our side no matter what we are going through. He holds us in the palm of His hand and takes care of our every need.

Knowing that God is always with us to comfort us is so important when changes are coming into our lives, like when we get new doctors. With a new diagnosis normally comes a new doctor. So many things to think about. So many questions to ask. So many questions you do not know to ask because, once again, you are stepping into the unknown. What will this do to my body? Will I be on medicine for it forever?

Praying the doctor joining your medical team is a Christian. Praying they are personable and will explain everything in terms that you can understand.

That is what happened to Tim and me as we walked into the world of endocrinology as I had mentioned earlier after I was diagnosed with severe hypothyroidism.

We were waiting in the waiting room to be called back. We obviously do a lot of that.

The nurse came to get us. She said the usual things the nurses say when they are taking you back to the doctor's room, but nowadays, it is hard to understand what they are saying through the mask required due to COVID.

We got back to the room. She asked the usual questions that we heard at all doctor visits. *Are you still using this pharmacy? Has there been any change in your medication? Do you have any pain today? Any nausea?* It was normal, routine stuff.

Before long, the atmosphere turned around completely. As she was asking the questions and seeing what we had gone through and were continuing to go through, she started making little comments. She was stunned at what we have dealt with.

Tim told her that I am writing my story, telling about how God is taking care of me and how He has been with us through it all. This opened the door to a beautiful visit.

"I hear You, God!"

Again, I believe He puts people in our path as a reminder of His love for us.

As our nurse shared a couple of stories with us about experiences she had with God, I literally had goose bumps up and down my arms and legs. We both had tears leaking from our eyes as His presence was so strongly felt in the room. I wish I could share her two stories with you, but those are hers to tell.

They were both incredibly beautiful and heartwarming. I will tell you that the power of God was proven again through her stories. She, Tim, and I all agree that we do not know how people get through life without Jesus Christ as their Savior.

After hearing her stories, I knew we were in the right place. There is no doubt that God put her there to remind me where the strength of my faith can lead, to remind me that He is the ultimate healer. It is the coolest thing ever when He places little reminders right in front of us to keep us strong and positive.

And for Dr. Cook, my new endocrinologist? We loved him. No, we did not have a God conversation with him, but he was the kind of doctor we want on our team. He even drew a picture on the whiteboard to illustrate what was going on with my thyroid. This gave me a clear understanding considering I am a visual, hands-on learner.

What do we do now? Get the new medicine regulated if needed. Wait and see. Since starting the medicine, I feel alive. I have actually made some of my own lunches and not slept all day. Trust me, that is a big deal!

Speaking of doctors...

I have the best medical team anybody could ask for. The best! When you are in a life-or-death situation and you feel at peace with the doctors who are taking care of you, you know you are in great hands; you are with the right people.

Dr. Miller and Dr. Levy have been phenomenal throughout this journey. I trust them both with every bit of my being. The biggest thing? They have heart. There is no doubt in my mind that they both care about me personally. I know that they both would do whatever it takes to keep me alive and as well as possible. That makes a special doctor.

In these days of "herd the patients through—the more patients that come through, the more money our health care system makes," neither of them has ever made me feel that way. Ever. They both take the time to listen—and as you can tell, I am a talker—and answer any questions Tim or I have. They make me feel safe. They make us both feel safe.

When you have this kind of team, you want to keep them by your side forever.

However, as my mama always told me, you do not always get what you want.

Dr. Miller, who is the most amazing oncologist on this planet, will be enjoying a very well-deserved retirement starting in a couple of months. I am more than happy for her. I really am! However, the selfish side of me is sad for her patients. She is the best and has been a lifesaver for me as well as many others. The new doctor may be taking her place professionally, but face it, no one will ever be able to fill her shoes. She is one of a kind.

Participating in the Stiletto Sprint for ovarian cancer awareness,
Deanna and her oncologist, Dr. Miller are having a blast!

Again—meeting a new doctor. Not just any doctor, but my oncologist—the one who will be going through this journey with me side by side, the one who will literally hold my life in her hands. How will she be? Is she a Christian? Does she believe in the power of God's healing? Will she truly care about me or will she herd me through like the system wants her to? Will her patients be able to build true relationships with her considering she is not even housed in Concord? Will she have a good bedside manner? Will she make me laugh? Is she personable? Will she do everything in her power to keep me alive? Will she look at me as a person—somebody's wife, mother, gramsie, daughter, friend instead of a number? Will she study my history and genuinely know my complicated case and all that comes with it? Will she keep an open dialogue with Dr. Levy? Will I be able to count on her to really, really care about me? *Will she have heart?*

I am grateful to say that I have now met my new oncologist, Dr. Brown, and I love her! From our very first meeting, she made me feel like I had known her forever. She made me feel comfortable. It was obvious through our conversation that she had learned my history and knew the direction we are heading toward. She took her time with me and answered all my questions. No, I do not know the answers to everything that I was wondering above, but I can honestly say that I feel in my heart that it is a perfect fit and that I am in good hands! I cannot wait for my family to meet her.

No matter what takes place in my life, I am determined to take the time to have fun while I can. I am determined to live the best life—make the greatest memories—and enjoy my family and friends. There is no way I would let all the negativity creep into my life without knocking it out with the good times! One of my favorite things? To be near water.

Toes in the sand, the sound of crashing waves, and the sun shining brightly on my face…it does not get much better than that. Ever since I was a little girl, the beach has always been one of my favorite places to visit.

Back in the day on our beach trips, it was all about the tan, going to the strip, the arcades, riding the rides, and oh yeah, do not forget checking out those good-looking guys! During our tween years through high school, my friend Beth and I would hit the beach first thing in the morning and stay all day long without a care in the world. Her parents took us every couple of weeks during the summer, so needless to say, we spent a lot of time there.

Those days are full of childhood memories that I will always cherish; however, as adults, we are creating new memories—memories that are life changing. Yes, I still like to lie in the sun; however, the rest of the things mentioned above are not even really thought about.

Now, our trips are simple but powerful. By that I mean just being able to sit on the beach is all I need. It makes me feel well. The difference that sitting by the ocean and breathing in the salt air makes with my health is amazing.

As I sit on the beach watching the movement of the water, I am reminded how mighty our God is. I am reminded that there is nothing that can come my way that I cannot handle with Him by my side; and I am reminded of the strength He gives to me to keep me going.

With her toes in the sand and the waves crashing
in, Deanna is loving her happy place!

Also sitting there in the sand gives me time to reflect on the many challenges that He has brought me through. I am truly a walking miracle because of Him.

Thankfully, my family and friends understand how important going to the beach is to me and they make sure I get there often.

Although Tim is more of a mountain man, he is always willing to spend time at the beach. A lot of mornings before I wake up, he will walk on the beach to find beautiful shells and shark teeth.

One year, without my knowing it, he started picking up this certain kind of shell. I do not know what they are called but they are small, round, and white. After collecting a good many of them, he showed them to me. He said they represent the purity of my body when the cancer is gone. I am telling you—he has the most thoughtful heart.

We brought those beautiful white shells home as well as many others. As a reminder of the trials we have made it through, the ones we are still having to battle, and our journey toward beating cancer to become as pure as the small white shells, I used the collection to create a display for us to see daily to help keep us focused on our goal.

Setting three jars together, I filled one with only the small white shells. The other two hold an assortment of shells. I added a cross that said BELIEVE and had a key attached. The variety of shells in the tall and medium jars represent everything that life throws at us. The challenges we have to deal with, just like the shells, come in all shapes and sizes. Some of them are rough, some are a little smoother, some are big, others are small. But…when we keep *believing* in Christ like the beautiful cross reminds us to do, we will find that it is the key to becoming much happier and much more at peace in our lives.

As a reminder of where they have been and where
they are going, Deanna used the shells Tim
found on the beach to create this display.

There are times when Tim stays home and I go the beach with my sisterfriends. They have stuck by my side since the very beginning and are willing to do whatever it takes to help me so I can go with them. I am definitely still independent but having me along can sometimes be extra—like ending up in the emergency room on one of our girls' beach trips as mentioned earlier. Even so, they never complain and give of themselves to make sure I am included in the fun.

Teenagers? Nope! It is a bunch of women in their
fifties having fun! Wende, Deanna, Denise, Michele,
Martha, and Tracy are living their best life!

It is not only the beach that makes me feel better. Having grown up with a family place at the lake, it played a big part in my life as well. There are so many memories from there—swimming, fishing, water skiing, riding in the boat, playing dolphins with my sissy, cooking what we caught, grilling good ol' hamburgers—the list goes on. My favorite memory is that my daddy was still alive then. I miss him terribly.

I love the lake so much. I have always wanted a place but knew it was not in our budget.

Like being by the ocean, being by the lake has a way of making me feel better.

My sissy, Beth, who lives at the lake now had been keeping her eyes open for us a place. It never hurts to dream, right? Well, she told us about a campground close to where she lives, so we decided to check it out.

Lake life! Beth and Deanna are cruising the lake on the jet ski.

From the very beginning, we decided if the lot was not on the water, we were not getting it. Plus before going to check it out, we had no idea of the rental price. In other words, it was all up in the air and more than likely, we were only dreaming.

Boy, I am glad she kept looking for us because our visit to the lake that day showed us another example of how God provides! There was one, yes, one lot left on the waterfront! Go, God!

When the owner showed it to us, I was getting really excited. I had high hopes. Oh, please let the price be right.

We could not believe what we were hearing. Not only was the price right, but the owner also knocked off another $250 for the year! My dream was finally coming true! We were getting a lot at the lake like I had always wanted.

Oh my goodness! It was wonderful! With the lake only being about thirty minutes from where we live, our family and friends were able to come often. My heart was happy as we made new memories—boat rides, making s'mores, cooking over the campfire, swimming, fishing, watching our grandbabies swing on the tree swing.

With all the lively action taking place, there were also calm and peaceful times when it was just Tim and me. One of my favorite things to do? Lie in the hammock, looking at the beauty around me while reflecting. Thank you, God, for giving us such a wonderful gift where we can be happy. Thank You for giving me joy in my heart. Thank You for giving our kids a place to come where we could make memories together that they would remember forever. Thank You for giving me a place to feel closer to my precious daddy.

Deanna is relaxing on the hammock at High Rock Lake.

Deanna's first love…her daddy, Bobby.
This picture was taken in the 80's.

The water. It has to be the water. Just like being at the beach, being by the lake affects the way I feel.

Tim and Deanna are sailing on a gorgeous
sunset cruise at the Outer Banks.

Another one of my favorite things to do is to go on road trips with my friends. There might be two of us, three of us, six of us—who knows. It just depends on whoever jumps in the car that weekend!

My sisterfriends, Denise and Wende, and I had been planning a trip to the beach for quite some time. That changed when the weather decided it did not want to cooperate with our plans.

It was on the news: a strong tropical cyclone, better known as a hurricane, will be making landfall at the beach on Thursday and continue inland. It was expected to cause catastrophic damage—winds over 80 mph; massive rainfall. People were boarding up their homes and evacuating. Businesses were boarded up and closed. Compare it to a ghost town. When did this happen? Just in time for our girls' road trip to the beach. We did not go, obviously, but we did not let it stop us.

We were still determined to take our trip. After discussing several different places to go instead of the beach, we could not make a decision; however, we did come up with a plan—a great one, I might add. The three of us decided to pack our bags for whatever might arise.

We went to an early dinner at a local restaurant to make our decision. With Wende's car packed and ready to go, we knew we could not go to the beach, so we needed to go in the opposite direction.

After throwing out several ideas, we still had not decided, so we each wrote on a piece of paper where we wanted to go most. We would draw one, and that was where we would go. Perfect plan, right? Yeah, that was what we thought too, but it did not quite work out that way. However, we did come to a conclusion. We would get into the car and head toward the mountains and whatever town we ended up in was where we would stay. No hotel reservations, no particular destination, just three girls on a road trip. Imagine that. It ended up being one of our favorite trips of all time, and let me tell you, Jesus really showed out that weekend!

After several hours on the road of talking, laughing, and having fun, we realized we were a little lost in the dark.

Tim texted to see if we had made it safely to wherever we were going. I always let him know when we do, but considering we were not there yet, I had not contacted him. We had more than enough time to get to wherever we were going.

"Uhhh, we are safe, but I cannot quite tell you where we are except for we are somewhere in the mountains trying to find a place to stop for the night. Honestly? We are lost."

Eventually, we saw a sign for Bryson City so we decided to go there for one night and move on the next day—again, not quite knowing where we would go.

As we were putting our luggage on the hotel's cart, it began to roll down the hill in the parking lot. Denise took off running after it. Thankfully, she caught it in time before it crashed!

By this trip, she had become a professional at chasing things. On one of our earlier trips, the wind decided it would steal our umbrella and swiftly take it down the beach. Before we knew it, she took off running after it, looking like one of the lifeguard babes from an old popular TV show! Even in her fifties, the girl can still run!

Bryson City was a great choice because it led us to riding the train through the Great Smoky Mountains. Before leaving to get on the train, we had a delicious breakfast at the hotel. During the meal, the lady working that area came over and began talking to us. In the conversation, she shared her story with us about her being a cancer survivor. That started our day out great. I love how Jesus puts people in my path to continually give me hope!

After breakfast, we hopped on the train, which proved to be an awesome experience. We loved seeing the beautiful scenery all around—trees, mountain streams, and (are you ready for this?) we even passed an incredibly gorgeous lake with houses on the water. Not on the shore by the water but sitting smack-dab in the middle of the water! A person would have to take a boat to get to them. Now, that is where I would like to visit sometime! It was immediately added to my bucket list!

After a couple of hours, the train stopped to let us off for lunch, giving us, I think, an hour and ten minutes to eat and get back on board to leave. They told us they would not wait on anybody.

Because I was having a hard time breathing and it was hard for me to walk very far on my own, I was using my wheelchair on this trip. Of course our train car—and it was a very long train—was the farthest from the restaurants so we were the last to get there, last to order, and…last to get back on the train.

The cars were all loaded and ready to go, except for three women—us. We had to hurry! We still had a little time, but not much.

Now, you have to picture this next scene. It was rather hilarious! Imagine this. The path to the train was all gravel. The three of us ladies—all in our fifties—were trying to make it back to the very last train car before it pulled off. Knowing there were only minutes to spare, Wende, who was pushing my wheelchair, shouted, "Hang on!"

She took off running while pushing me down the gravel path with Denise running behind her. I am sure that looked pretty funny to the people who were sitting on the train.

Now, you may think I had it easy riding in the wheelchair. Oh no, not at all. My whole body, every single inch of it, was bobbing around like a bobblehead while I clutched tightly to the armrests hoping she did not hit too big of a bump and throw me out flat on my face! We were laughing the whole way! Believe me, it was a long run, but whew, we made it with two minutes left on the clock. They were exhausted from running. Me? I was just laughing with them!

After we got back into our seats, this sweet lady came over to us and asked me if she could pray with me. I love when random people do that. I feel like Jesus puts them close to me for a reason. We were sitting on long, benchlike seats that went down the middle of the car, so she had to lean over both of my friends to get to me, acknowledging them with a grin. She said the sweetest prayer and said the most caring words to me. I was very grateful for her kindness. I want to make that clear, but afterward, my friends and I were tickled. It had become a joke with us that since I had my head shaved, nobody noticed them. People would come up and speak to me when we were out together but never acknowledge them, as if they were invisible. The lady on the train did at least give them a grin. Again, I was very grateful for her, but it was funny that she leaned over them both to get to me.

After the train ride, we continued our unplanned journey with no idea of where we would end up next, where we would stay, nothing. We came to a fork in the road: to the left, Pigeon Forge; to the right, Gatlinburg.

"Which way?"

"It doesn't matter."

"I don't care."

"Y'all tell me!"

Still no answer. It came down to where a choice had to be made, and at the same time, Denise and I said, "You choose!" Wende whipped the car to the right and off to Gatlinburg we went! That would be our home for the next couple of days.

Now we had to find a place to stay. Denise and I searched the Internet for cabins and hotels while Wende drove us around. We arrived at a place that, even though it had three floors, had "motel" in the name. I had always told Tim I would not stay in a motel because, to me, most of them looked sketchy. A hotel, yes; a motel, no.

Denise went into the office and checked it out. The price was right, but we were still uncertain. As we drove through the parking lot, there was a nice-looking couple getting out of their car. We stopped and asked the lady about the place. She said she loved it and that they had stayed there for thirty years. She told us that it was very clean and everything inside was vintage—down to the white cotton bedspreads.

We decided that was where we would stay. She was right. It was great! When we walked into our room, it felt as if we were stepping back in time. Everything was clean as a whistle. It even smelled fresh. There, lying on the desk, was an open Bible. You do not see that anywhere anymore. One of the best perks? It was located on a side road of the main strip, so we never had to move the car once it was parked.

Every time we left the motel to head to the strip, we passed a pizza place with the biggest pizza we had ever seen in our lives in the window of the restaurant. I believe they said it was thirty inches in diameter! I knew I had to have some of that before we left.

Pizza in Gatlinburg comes BIG! Deanna
had no problem eating every bite!

Gatlinburg was wonderful! I loved everything about it. I loved the sights, the sounds, the food, and being there with my friends.

Deanna and her sisterfriends, Denise and Wende, take a quick minute for a photo op in Gatlinburg.

I did, however, learn of new feelings. I learned what it was like to have part of my independence taken away. Going down the sidewalk or in and out of shops in a wheelchair was not the easiest thing to do. Someone else other than myself was responsible for getting me from point A to point B. When I wanted to look at something, I had to ask to be pushed over to where the item was. It was not a good feeling at all.

I was thankful for my wheelchair, though, and for my friends, who were willing to do all the work of pushing me around everywhere. Without them and the chair, I would not have been able to do things we did. I was grateful. It was just that I felt like a part of me was gone, and I wanted it back. I wanted to breathe normally—to walk without getting out of breath. I wanted to choose where I went without having to ask someone to push me there. I wanted to be *me*! *Me*, the independent person I had always been.

That night, while we were enjoying the excitement of the strip, a lady and her son came up to me to ask if she could pray for me. Absolutely. We all bowed our heads while she said the sweetest prayer of healing over me.

Better yet, in my eyes, she was setting an incredible example for her son. How great it was for him to see his Christian mother walking up to a complete stranger and praying for her. She was definitely walking the walk and teaching her child, maybe without realizing it, how to love others and share Jesus's love. I am telling you, like I said earlier, Jesus was really showing out that weekend. Everywhere we turned, He had placed little reminders of His love for us to see.

The Gatlinburg story cannot be told without the loud "snores" being included. So, we were in our motel room. My two sisterfriends, Denise and Wende, who claim to love me so much, threatened to make me sleep in the bathtub because of how loudly I snored the night before. I told them to give me some pillows to lie on and blankets to cover up with and I would do it. Of course they were playing around. Well, maybe they were, maybe they were not. Anyway, Wende and I were in one bed and Denise was in the other. ZZZZZZzzzzz, ZZZZZZzzzzz. Super, super loud—ZZZZZZzzzzz, ZZZZZZzzzzz.

Tim had been telling me that I had been snoring at home. I did not believe him. He recorded me so I could hear it. Well, Wende did the same thing at the motel. She wanted me to hear how I sounded.

After not being able to sleep for the second night because of the horrific noises, she got out of my bed and got in the other bed with Denise. The story I heard the next morning was that she had grabbed her pillow, told Denise to move over, and crawled in bed with her. She told Denise to tell me to turn over so I would quit snoring. Denise looked over at me and then back at Wende.

"She is turned over."

We asked her if she thought it would be any quieter from that bed, considering the size of the motel room. Now, you have to visualize the dramatics that went with this story. Remember, she was frustrated because she could not sleep; plus, you had to see how funny Denise was reenacting it.

They told me it was not a regular snore, that it sounded like it was coming from my throat, which is exactly what I told Tim when I heard his recording. I told him and them that something was not right in my throat. You had to hear the recordings. I sounded dreadful, and that is not exaggerating. It was not a regular snore. It was one of the worst things I have ever heard! I literally sounded like an old cow—think a deep-down, loud moooo-mooo! Not a wimpy little moo but an extra-loud, extra-deep one. *That* is what it sounded like! Seriously!

No wonder it was keeping everybody awake.

After I got home, we discovered where this "mooing" was coming from. Unfortunately, my vocal cords had become paralyzed from the double stroke I had earlier—one on each side of my brain—that we thought had left no residual. This stroke experience was in addition to the one I told you about in the beginning of my story. We also learned that the shortness of breath we thought was a side effect from the chemo was also caused by my vocal cords becoming paralyzed. So now, not only were we dealing with cancer and strokes, we were dealing with paralyzed vocal cords that would not let air pass easily because they were almost closed.

At the time, we decided we were going to keep living life like we had been. If the snoring or breathing started to get worse, I was to call my Dr. Langford, my ENT doctor.

A few months passed, and we lived life as usual—until early Christmas morning. Out of a sound sleep, I sat straight up and was gasping for every breath. It scared both of us. Tim quickly helped me get dressed and took me to the emergency room. The closer we got to the hospital, the worse it got.

As soon as we got there, they put me in a room and started giving me oxygen. It seemed like nurses and doctors came in from everywhere checking everything about me. They were being very thorough and decided to admit me to the ICU2 unit.

Dr. Lankford was out of town, so the ENT on call at the hospital came in to see me. We loved her. She told me that I would need to have a tracheal tube put in to help with my breathing. I was devastated. This could not be happening. I was seriously not getting a trach. Oh, yes, I was.

The doctor told me that we would not have to do it right then but it would need to be done. In my mind, I was thinking maybe months down the road. I asked her if she had any idea when that might be. Her response?

"Tomorrow."

There went the tears. There went the air out of my sails. I did not know what to think. I mean, I knew it had to be done, but I did not want that thing sticking out of my throat. I did not want to have to depend on it to breathe. Was there no other way to take care of this? No. That was it. I was going to have it put in the next day. I felt like I had just been punched in the stomach.

Tim was there to hold me. There is something special about his touch that gives me comfort. All he has to do is touch my arm or hold my hand or wrap his arms around me, and I feel at peace. Thankfully, he was by my bedside when the doctor gave me that news.

We were very grateful that a nurse who was looking through my records noticed that I was on a blood thinner, so they had to hold off on the surgery for several days. They had to let the medication get out of my system so I would not bleed out during surgery.

The doctor told us she could not, in good conscience, let me go home in the shape I was in. Then—*then*—I realized how serious this actually was. There we sat in ICU2 unable to go home because I could possibly die.

The next five days were spent waiting for the upcoming surgery. Family and friends visited and kept my spirits up, even though I was constantly on the verge of crying the whole time. A few tears did slip out during some visits even though I tried my best to stay strong.

The windowsill in my room was full of Christmas gifts, cards, pictures, and other goodies.

We had the best nurses we could ever ask for. One young nurse brought in inspirational signs that read "You're strong," "You're beautiful," "Keep the faith," plus about five more that she had taken the time to make herself. The fact that she cared enough to make these daily reminders for me to keep my spirits up meant the world to us both. Another nurse brought me a soft and cuddly stuffed animal and a bag of snacks. That animal (even though to this day we have not quite figured out what it is) was my comfort. Soothing. Just to hold it made me feel more at ease. It stayed in my arms the whole time I was there except for when I was in surgery. I have actually taken it back to the hospital for stays after that one. Funny how much comfort a stuffed animal can bring.

Deanna found comfort in snuggling with her pink thing-a-ma-jig that her nurse gave her during an eleven-day hospital stay.

I had two main questions for the doctor. Was it going to be permanent? After the initial period, would I be able to talk with it? I wanted to continue sharing my story of what Jesus was doing in my life. I did not want that taken away. I wanted people to know how amazing He is and how He would work in their lives too.

Permanent or not? We did not know. It was a wait-and-see game. As far as speaking, there should be no problems after the first day or so.

Our daughter, Megan, who is in the military and was deployed at the time, texted me during my stay and told me she had a surprise for me. A few minutes later, I heard a knock on the door.

"Come in."

"Hey, Mama!"

Oh, my goodness! I was so excited!

It was Destiny, one of Megan's best friends whom I had not seen in a couple of years. Her husband was also in the military, and they were living out of town. Even though she was only home for a few days, she took the time to help Megan surprise me with a vanilla milkshake!

This made my day! First, because that was thoughtful of our baby girl. Second, because I got to see her sweet friend, who I love dearly; and third, because I love vanilla milkshakes!

Within a day or two, while we were still waiting to have the surgery, we were watching TV and heard the worst news ever. We learned that the area where our daughter was deployed to was being bombed. Oh, the feelings. I am not even sure how to explain them. I know she is an adult, but to us, she will always be our little girl. I know she chose to be there, but that does not help a mama who loves her daughter more than she could ever imagine. Knowing she was in that mess and there was not a thing we could do to help her was crushing me. Believe me, Tim and I were both doing some serious praying.

There we were—me lying in bed, Tim by my side in the recliner—waiting to have a surgery that was going to save my life, and that came on TV. Can you imagine?

Megan was supposed to be coming home around that time but got delayed because of the bombing. Thankfully, she did eventually make it home safely.

Lots of happy tears are flowing as Megan
returns home safely from deployment.

The big day came. Dr. Langford was back in town, so he would be doing the surgery. I asked him if he was ready to slit my throat. I thought he was going to fall over. You have to laugh at these things; if not, there would be way too many tears. My sweet husband prayed with me as he does before any procedure.

Everything went well in the operating room. Recovery went well. I was back in ICU2 for a couple of days before being moved to a regular room.

I had no voice after surgery, which was expected in the beginning. This should have only lasted a day or two. My friend Alisha had brought us whiteboards and markers so we could communicate during this time. Great idea! The funny thing was, in the beginning, nurses, therapists, etc., would come in asking me questions as if I could answer. Thank goodness for the whiteboards so I could!

When other people were talking in the room, it felt like I was in a box. The whole world was going on around me, and I was just there. Do not get me wrong, I was included in conversations; I just could not write as fast as I could speak to join in. Everybody was patient and waited for me to finish writing. I guess the bottom line is I just wanted to be normal. I just wanted to be me. My emotions were on edge. I prayed, asking Jesus to please let me speak again.

Late one evening, almost midnight, I started having a horrible coughing spell. Because the nasty secretion was coming from my chest, my nurse had to come in and do a deep suction with the catheter. A deep suction is when they run the catheter into my trach down to the top of my lungs. It is horrible. Depending on how bad the secretions are, this may have to be repeated more than once in a sitting.

This particular night happened to be New Year's Eve. Yep—we spent Christmas in the hospital, and we were still there ringing in the New Year.

The nurse that was in the room with us did what she needed to do as far as using the catheter, and, of course, this was one of those times it needed to be done twice. Before doing it a second time, she stopped and waited, considering both hands on the clock were about to strike twelve. With only a few seconds to go, this gave the three of us the opportunity to watch the ball drop on television, but most importantly, it gave Tim the chance to kiss me at midnight like he had done for the past twenty-five years.

After we rung in the New Year, the nurse finished doing what she had to do. Hopefully, this unique entrance into 2020 will be a once in a lifetime New Year experience.

The following day, Dr. Langford came in to deflate the trach cuff and put on my speaking valve so I could talk. I could not wait to talk again!

Deflated cuff. Check. Speaking valve on. Check. Talking. Did not happen. Take off the valve. No voice. My vocal cords were still swollen from the surgery.

Will I ever be able to speak again? I wrote on my whiteboard. He told me I should be fine when the swelling goes down. I asked him what would happen if the swelling did not go away. We all know how that went. I was so upset.

At the time, Tim; two of my cousins, Diane and Kim; my "second daughter," Kayla; and two of my teacher friends, Elizabeth and

Georgann (one being a speech therapist) were all in the room. In other words, we had a full house. Jesus had placed the perfect people in the room at the perfect time.

Kayla asked for my phone. She put an app on it that would speak for me. I just typed in what I wanted to say, and it would say it for me. Elizabeth, my friend the speech therapist, talked about the possibility of getting a speech-generating device, although it cost thousands of dollars. Diane and Kim told me not to worry, that I would have whatever I needed. If it was the device, I would get it. They said they would do fundraisers or whatever was needed to get it for me.

Tim called our kids to update them on what was going on. They were willing to take a sign language class. I had so much love and support.

Even though I was surrounded by so much love and such caring hearts, I was devastated at the news I had just gotten. If I cannot ever speak again, how was I going to share my story? How was I going to let people know of the miracles Jesus had done and continued to do in my life? I wanted people to know that He was still in the miracle-making business and that He would take care of them like He had been taking care of me! I was trying so hard to stay positive. For the rest of that evening, still nothing. No voice. *Jesus, please let the swelling go down.*

The next morning, we waited on the Dr. Langford to come back so I could try again. Several hours later, he came by and put on the speaking valve once again. *I was doing it!* The swelling had gone down, and *I was talking!* I remember the nurse saying, "Look at that face!"

I remember having the most incredible feeling in the world when I heard my voice! It was quiet, weak, and raspy, but at least there was sound coming out! Prayers were answered! I am telling you all. Jesus is great! He hears our prayers!

I was so, so, so grateful! The speaking valve took a little time to get used to, but without it, I could not speak at all. It took weeks for my voice to become stronger, but with God's grace, it did.

During that eleven-day hospital stay, we had to learn a whole new lifestyle with this trach and what to do once we went home.

It required daily cleanings plus suctioning out secretions—nasty mucus coming out of the hole in my neck, my trach, and my nose—all at the same time in the beginning. This was caused by horrible coughing spells that would also make my head hurt and cause me to spit up from being choked. Something as small as changing positions would throw me into a spell.

Tim had to learn how to do the suctions with the yonker and also the catheter. Yes, he had to run the catheter through my trach down to the top of my lungs. A representative from the medical supply company had come by my room before we were to be discharged and showed Tim how to use the equipment we would have to have at home for trach care. There was so much to learn. When he was there, so were two of my friends, Georgann and Kim. I had already told them that everything was so confusing to me that I relied on my husband to know what to do. Well, when the rep was there explaining everything, I could see it on their faces.

"Now you know why I depend on him. It is all so confusing."

They both agreed that they still would not know what to do after hearing the representative.

Luckily, the doctor who was on call the day we were supposed to go home asked if we would like to stay another day and let Tim learn how to do everything hands on. The nurses could guide him through what needed to be done so he would know exactly what he was doing. Boy! That was another answer to prayer because they were sending us home with no proper training. The equipment training did not teach him how far to go down in my chest while suctioning, among other things.

Because there was so much to this new trach deal, we went to my husband's parents' home so his mother could help, just like we did after my hysterectomy.

Oh my goodness! When we got there, the equipment had been delivered. I am not kidding when I say it took up almost the length of the wall in the bedroom and was stacked almost chest high! There were three machines as well as boxes and boxes of supplies that I would be needing. That was only a month's worth. We would have to order the same the following month and every month after. All of this for the low price of only $2,750…a month! Thankfully, we had insurance, which did bring it down to the lower hundreds a month. That was not easy either, but it was much better than in the thousands. Plus, we had to buy a nebulizer, which made it four machines I would be using. Believe me, it took two people to do all that needed to be done. I started calling my husband Dr. Tim and my precious mother-in-law Nurse Mary. They did so much to keep me alive.

"Nurse Mary," Tim's mama, telling us she loves us!

Also when we got home, we were visited twice a week by home health care and a speech therapist. These services lasted for several weeks. A community paramedic also came by to let us know the service they provided. He told us that if we have to call 911, the service would show that there was a trach patient in the home so they would know to get there quickly.

Our home health nurse was awesome. She made sure we had what we needed and of course checked my vitals each time. Tim did everything she did except listen to my heart and lungs with the stethoscope. The speech therapist was a great lady too, but she said from the very beginning that she did not feel like I needed speech. She came the times she was assigned and then signed off.

Our nurse called one day and said that she received a call saying they wanted to continue home health care, speech therapy, and physical therapy for me. What? It was already decided I did not need speech, plus I never had physical therapy to begin with. In reality, I did not need home health care either. She agreed with me, so we stopped all home services. I really hated to see her go because she was a lot of fun! You know, someone you feel like you have known all your life when you first meet them, someone you would like to hang out with?

In the beginning, the suctioning was happening often and close together. My nose was pouring. I went through box after box of tissues. Tim and Mary would have to keep emptying the trash can beside the bed because I used so many tissues.

Some suctions could be done at the edge of my trach with the yonker and some had to be deep with a catheter. I really do not like to speak negatively, but this experience was absolutely, positively horrible. I truly felt like it was worse than what I had been experiencing with cancer.

We were getting up probably five or six times a night at first for Tim to use the suction machine on me. The secretion would build up in my chest to the point that I would start coughing horribly, which caused me to struggle with my breathing. That would wake us both up. He would suction out my trach and then a little later it would happen again. It seemed like the least little movement would cause us to have to use the suctioning machine.

Using the yonker was not bad, just annoying because it was so often. Now, having to have a deep suction? Oh. My. Goodness. It was terrible. I dreaded every time he had to do it, and I know he did too. Tears would stream down my face, my nose would run even more, my face would turn blood-red, and I could not breathe for a couple of seconds. I would not wish it on anybody.

In addition to the main suction machine, we had one for travel. Once we started going out some, we had to take it everywhere we went, along with a bag of supplies, in the event I needed to be suctioned while we were gone.

Also, when we first got home from the hospital, I had to stay in the bed or sit in the chair beside the bed almost twenty-four hours every day because I had to be hooked up to a moisturizing compressor. I had a long blue tube running from my throat to the machine. This helped keep the secretions moist and prevent them from clotting up. The only time I could come off the machine was to eat, shower, go to the bathroom, or get a breathing treatment, which caused me to be hooked up to my nebulizer—yet another machine.

After several weeks of this, Dr. Langford said I could come off the moisturizing compressor during the day and only sleep with it on. Let me tell you, this machine is loud. Of course, we were used to the noise by then so it was no biggie, but it was loud. I was so thankful to get a break from being hooked up to it almost all day long. It was liberating not to have some kind of machine hooked up to my body.

Patti, Debbie, Denise, Kim, Deanna, and Georgann
are having fun just like they did in high school!

Close to a year after finding out my vocal cords were paralyzed and about six months of having the trach put in, I heard Dr. Langford say these beautiful words.

"Your voice is really strong. It sounds like your vocal cords are working again."

"Really? Does that mean we get to take the trach out?"

"Let's give them another month. We'll leave it in till our next visit and I'll check them then."

Oh my goodness! I was so excited! Of course I did not *want* to wait another month. I *wanted* it out that day, but I was more than willing if it meant the possibility of getting this thing out of my throat! If waiting another month would give my vocal cords the chance to grow stronger, yes, I would be glad to wait.

The next visit came. Tim had to sit in the truck because of the COVID restrictions. I went in by myself, waiting to hear the words I longed for.

"Deanna."

There it was. The nurse called my name. What was he going to say? Would I get the trach out? Had my vocal cords really started working again on their own? That in itself is a miracle!

I could not wait to get into his office to find out.

Dr. Langford ran the long, skinny, tubelike camera up through my nose all the way down my throat—or at least it felt like it went that far. I am not sure how far it went. Gag. Gag. Oh, man! I was hoping I was not going to throw up all over him. That would have been awful!

Then came the news…one vocal cord was working, the other was only barely moving. The good news? It was working enough for us to take out the trach! I was out-of-this-world excited!

With me being the positive thinker I am, I tried not to think about the fact that Dr. Langford made me fully aware that there was a possibility of the trach having to be put back in even though I knew it in my heart. I focused on the fact that it was out and that I did not have to depend on it to breathe anymore.

I could not wait to get out to the truck and show Tim. Look, honey—no trach!

For the next week or so, I had to keep silk tape over the hole in my throat. When I ate, drank, or spoke, I had to squeeze the hole together to make sure nothing came out. I needed it to stay together so the skin would grow together and close up. It was the best feeling ever! The trach was out, and before long, my neck would be normal again.

Unfortunately, as I have said so many times before, Tim and I never know from one minute to the next what is going to happen in our life. This next story is a perfect example of that. Only seventeen days after having my trach taken out...

Bedtime. Tim checked my oxygen level. Ninety-seven. All good.

Within ten minutes of lying down to watch TV, I sat straight up in the bed with this horrifying sound coming out of me because I could not catch my breath.

Tim and I locked eyes—both with scared looks on our faces. What in the world?

"Are you okay?"

I could not answer.

"Deanna."

I was trying so hard, but it kept getting worse. I could not say a thing.

He helped me out of the bed and into the bathroom. Hoping to find something that would help, I splashed water on my face.

Oh...the fear I saw on my face when I looked into the mirror. A look that will forever be etched in my mind.

That did not work. I was thinking fresh air might help so he helped me get outside to sit on the porch, hoping for the best. I knew I was grasping at straws, but I was trying to think of anything and everything that would help me breathe.

Calling 911 and trying to help me at the same time, Tim stayed right by my side. Things were only getting worse. It was the deepest, loudest, most horrific sound we had ever heard. In fact, when the 911 dispatcher heard the noise over Tim's phone, she asked, *"Is that her?"*

I could not breathe. I say that, but I had to be taking in some breath because I am still alive today.

Honestly, though, I thought I was going to meet God that night.

I knew that if I did not get help soon, that was exactly where I was headed. There was no doubt in my mind. Saying I was terrified is an understatement. I was not terrified of dying, because when I die, I know I am going to heaven, but I was terrified of what was happening at the time. I was gasping for every breath with little to no success.

Later, Tim told me he was thinking the same thing as it was happening. Helpless, there was nothing he could do except what he did, and that was call 911 and pray. We were both praying. In fact, I was begging God in my mind.

Please, oh, please, God, please help me!

I was begging so hard. I had never been so scared in my life. This time was much worse than the first time when I had been in a similar situation. It was in God's hands whether I lived or died that night.

The dispatcher stayed on the line with Tim while we waited on the emergency workers to get to the house. Trying my best to get it out, I was pushing the words, "Tell...them...to...hurry." It was only halfway understandable, but he knew what I was saying. If they did not, I was going to die.

I started to get my breath little by little, not fully, but it was beginning to improve. Then a tiny bit more—still struggling but catching a small break.

Oh, thank You, God! Thank You! Thank You! Thank You!

It was not long before I started losing it again. I never lost it as bad as in the beginning, but I felt the horror returning. I started begging again.

Please, God, help me breathe!

Again, little by little, my breath started coming back.

What felt like forever, but was only a few minutes, the sirens of the firetruck were within hearing distance, then we could see the lights coming our way. Oh, thank You, Jesus, they were turning onto our road and were there to take care of me.

Slowly, I began to breathe better and better after the firefighters arrived. They checked my vitals. Everything looked good. I was fighting tears because that only made it worse.

Then came more sirens and lights. It was the paramedics. By the time they arrived, my breathing, although a little short, was close to normal.

God had done it again! He answered prayer and put the right people in front of me to give me the help I needed to keep me alive!

They asked me if I wanted to go to the hospital. Absolutely. I am telling you, I felt like I had been knocking on death's door. There was no way I was not going to get checked out because if it happened again that night, I might not make it through.

One of the hardest things was pulling off in that ambulance and leaving Tim behind. He was sitting on the front porch watching us leave. I knew his heart was breaking, and there was not a thing I could do. I could see it in his face. Mine was breaking too because he would not be with me. I was scared. He was scared. We needed each other.

This was happening during the time of the COVID pandemic, so visitors were not allowed at the hospital. Watching him watch us pull away broke my heart. I was going to have to go this one alone.

Upon arriving, I was taken straight into a room and the tests began. Scan, EKG, X-ray, etc.

Just what we had expected, but definitely not wanted, the doctor on call let me know that they were discussing putting my trach back in.

No! It had been only seventeen days that I was breathing on my own. *Seventeen days* of freedom! I did not want to have that thing put back in my neck. Please, oh, please. Please, not the trach. I did not want to go back into surgery again. I had just had three hernias removed a few weeks earlier. Maybe they did not know what they were talking about since none of them was an ENT. Maybe they were wrong. Maybe I will not have to get it back. I was holding on to hope.

The results of the tests started coming in. *What?* No way. Absolutely, no way. No possible way. A heart attack? If so, it was a very mild one. Rare aggressive cancer, multiple strokes, paralyzed vocal cords, a trach, and now the possibility of having the trach put back in *plus* a heart attack? All in three and a half years? Not to mention pneumonia, a hysterectomy, hernia surgery, sepsis, neutropenia, neuropathy—the list goes on. When would I get a break? It has been one thing after another!

We had made it through everything else; we did not have a choice except to make it through these things too. I just wished Tim would have been there holding me when they gave me that news.

According to test results, troponin enzymes were released from my heart, which told them it may have been a heart attack. After running more tests, they learned that the enzymes were released because of the stress of me not being able to breathe. It was not a heart attack after all. Even though the stress put on my heart was obviously not good, at least it was not a heart attack.

As every adventure to the emergency room ends of for me, I was admitted because of my health history. I was told I would be going to ICU2 so they could keep a close eye on me, but that did not happen.

First stop after the emergency room? Instead of ICU2, I was placed in a holding room on the observation floor where they automatically put all patients who were waiting on their COVID test results. For every patient who came in, they did a swab for the test. The results of the test would depend on the floor I would be moved to next.

When the nurse told me that was where I would be going, I told him there was no way. No way could I be on that floor. I could not share a bathroom with another patient. Yes, our hospital still has one section of rooms where patients share bathrooms with one another.

Cancer. Never, ever should a cancer patient with a compromised immune system share a bathroom in the hospital with anybody, especially when it is considered the holding floor for patients waiting on results for their COVID testing. Yep! You've got it: the same virus that shut our country down—no, that shut the world down. No, not a place for cancer patients.

Yes. They were still sending me to that floor. Why? Why could they not understand that I could not go on that floor? I would not share a bathroom with anybody. I refused. Call my oncologist. She will tell you that I cannot go there. I was getting myself all worked up over nothing.

My ER nurse did exactly what I had asked him to do. Even though some of the rooms did share a bathroom, there were also private rooms. He had arranged for me to have my own room to keep me safe. When I arrived at the room, I discovered that my nursing assistant happened to be the mother of our daughter's friend. She told me when she saw my name, she told them then that they needed to change my room. She explained my situation and made sure I had what I needed. Thankfully, I had two people there making sure I was well taken care of.

With the eventful night that caused the hospital visit, I will be honest, I was afraid to go to sleep. I was up all night the first night it happened and then again the second night. If I had fallen asleep, I did not know if I would wake up. Wishing I could sleep, I just could not.

Being around me, it will not take long to know that I talk about my husband a lot. He is my rock. I was really missing him. After determining that I did not have the virus, my sweet nurse arranged it so he could come to the hospital and be with me. The hospital still had restrictions in place but allowed visitors in certain cases. With him by my side, it was not long till I dozed off. I knew I was safe.

Do not get me wrong, the nurses were great, but they also had their hands full with other patients. Even when a patient hits the call button, they were not always at liberty to come right then considering they were short-staffed, through no fault of theirs. We had been to the hospital enough to know that.

However, because of my situation at the time, I was told by the doctor on call that the nurses were told that if I hit the call button to drop what they were doing and get to my room fast. We all knew what would happen if they did not. With my husband being there, if anything had happened, I was at peace knowing he would be able to get immediate help if I needed it. The doctor on call thought it was a great idea having him there because it gave him another set of eyes to watch me.

While on the observation floor, Dr. Langford came to see me. With me gagging the whole time, he ran the camera up my nose and down my throat to find out that my vocal cords, once again, had stopped working properly. Even though my speech was strong, my breathing was not. The emergency doctors guessed right. I was going to have the trach put back in.

On the third day of my stay, I was moved from the observation floor to the family medicine floor, for a few short hours anyway—just long enough for a different doctor on call to come by. We were hoping my husband would get to stay with me there with no problems. He did. This doctor also agreed that it was best that he be there with me.

Before we knew it, they were moving me to ICU2. Dr. Langford said he could put the trach back in the next day; however, that was not possible because I was on a blood thinner and had to be off it for at least five days so I would not bleed out in the operating room. This was the same thing that happened the first time I had to have the trach put in. He let us know that he could not let me go home till after the surgery because of the seriousness of my situation.

We stayed in ICU2 for the next couple of days and then we were moved to the new heart floor. The heart floor? Why were we being moved there? It freed up my room in ICU2 for someone else. Another reason was that the heart floor has their own intensive care unit. My room was close to it in case I had an emergency; their doctors could get to me quickly.

Thank goodness we got to stay on this floor the remainder of our ten-day stay. We loved it! The nurses were great to Tim and me both. He actually had a pull-out bed that he could sleep on instead of cramping up in a recliner. Let me tell you, he has been a trooper sleeping on those recliners for the past several years. I was grateful he would be more comfortable.

Up until time for the surgery, I tried my hardest to come up with every possible reason that could have caused my breathing troubles—reasons that would not cause me to have the trach replaced. It did not work. It was getting replaced. Even though I could not stand the thought of having to have the trach back, I knew it was the only way I would be able to stay alive. If I wanted to live, I had to have it.

I did not like the thought of Tim having to do all of the caretaking he had done in the past. The daily cleaning, the changing of the cannulas twice a day, the suctioning, the deep suctioning, the monthly ordering of supplies. He never complained at all, but to me, he had already done so much for me that getting rid of the trach had to be a relief for him.

Dr. Langford told us that we should be able to start where we left off when the first trach was taken out, which was a good thing. That meant that the secretions would not be as horrible as they were in the beginning. Thank goodness he was right. Yes, we have had to use the suction machines but not every couple of hours like we did the first time. I still have coughing spells—oh, I am so tired of them—but they are not as severe and do not happen as often. I am ready for the coughing to be over—done—zilch—out of here.

Because the hole in my throat from the first trach had already grown shut, I had to go into surgery again to have the trach put back in.

Second tracheostomy. New hole in my throat. New trach. Recovery. Back in my room.

Here we go again. I could not talk. We knew it would be a couple of days, but this time, it went a little longer than that. I knew in my heart that I would talk again, but there was that little piece of me that could not help but wonder. By then, Tim was really good at understanding what I was trying to say when I could not say anything at all. He understood my signals; he was becoming a pro at interpreting my motions.

Although I was thankful for the speaking app that Kayla had put on my phone the first go-around so I could "speak" to the doctors and nurses when they came in, I was ready to be able to use my own voice.

Finally, I could hear me—my own voice, me speaking. To me, that in itself was a miracle. When you go from having surgery to get a trach because your vocal cords are paralyzed, to not being able to speak because the surgery caused your vocal cords to swell, and then being able to speak within days? That is a miracle!

While most people spend time with family or take vacations on holidays, we seemed to be spending them all in the hospital during the first half of 2020, considering this particular visit was our third "holiday visit" of the year. Actually, our second of the current year. We were in there Christmas and New Year's Eve of 2019, then New Year's Day and Fourth of July 2020. We could hear fireworks going off all around us but could not see any from my window. To "celebrate," we watched a firework show on TV; that was as close to real as we could get. We were together—that was all that really mattered to us.

After this hospital visit, we came home to our house. "Dr. Tim" was a pro at taking care of me by then. He knew all the ins and outs of trach care.

Daily, Tim cleans Deanna's trach.

There was one thing that was a little irritating. Each morning when he cleaned my trach, there was a little sore spot that he would hit. It was behind the actual trach, so it was not easily visible to the eye. When he saw it, it was a tiny piece of skin hanging out of the hole the trach was in.

When I went for my follow-up visit with Dr. Langford, I told him about it. He checked it out and said it was granulated tissue. He had to cauterize it. He told me that it may have to be done a second time and it did. I do not care to have my neck burned again. Ever.

It has been four years. Four years of changing physically, mentally, emotionally, socially, and spiritually. Four years of the unknown. Four years of one diagnosis after another. Four years of living on an emotional roller coaster. Four years of everything being fine one minute to having to be admitted to the hospital the next. Four years of facing death multiple times…

How have I handled all of this? Not alone. My God has been by my side every step of the way. He has worked miracle after miracle to keep me alive.

And here on earth? He has given me close family and friends to listen to me when I need to talk or even cry, to hold me when I need to be held, and to laugh with me to keep my spirits high. He has also given me angels on earth.

Angels on earth. Just by reading those three little words, you probably already know who I am talking about. You are right! I am talking about my amazing oncology nurses, the ones in the clinic, the ones in the lab, and the ones on the oncology floor of the hospital.

I have learned that people have to have a loving heart to be nurses. In my experience, I have also learned that a lot of them love Jesus too, which is very comforting to me. No, I do not ask them; it is just obvious by their actions and our conversations. Of course, I have been around nurses all my life, but having gone through the experiences that I have over the past four years, I have a different perspective of them. Saying that they are amazing is an understatement.

In the clinic, the nurses are the first people you see once you have checked in. They set the tone before you even see the doctor. At our hospital, I have always had kind calming ladies from the very first step through the door. You can only imagine how important this is considering you are walking into that office as a basket case right after your whole world gets turned upside down. You have no idea what your future holds or if you are even going to live or die.

The first time at the clinic when one of the nurses had to access my port to draw blood, I made a big mistake. For some crazy reason, I glanced over right before she was about to stick me with the needle. In my head, I thought, she is about to poke me with a four-inch nail! No, the needle did not really look like a four-inch nail. It was not that long or big around. That was just my mind playing tricks on me when I saw it for the first time. Now? My port has been accessed so many times that I am used to it and it is no big deal. I just do not look at the needle anymore!

Along with the nurses in the clinic are my lab nurses. They are definitely special people. These visits begin with the girls that take my vitals and then walk me back to my cubby where I get my treatment. Like the nurses in the clinic, these girls set the tone. The two of them are always upbeat and happy, which starts the visit out on a good note.

Once I am in my cubby, that is what I call the little space where I sit, I have one nurse who is assigned to administer my medication and take care of me. I can honestly say—and I think this is a big deal—that Tim and I have loved every nurse I have had. I say it is a big deal because we have been going for over four years and think about it, that is a long time to hit the jackpot on the people taking care of you. You would think that every now and then you might have somebody you are not sure of, but not at our hospital. I can honestly say that we have been very pleased with them all.

As far as my stay in the lab, it is normally anywhere from two to five hours. The length of time depends on the type of chemotherapy drug that I am getting and whether my lab work is taken on that day or prior to that visit. It was always taken on the day of treatment until COVID hit. Now I have to go a couple days before treatment to get swabbed for the virus and to have my lab work done. Yes, I have to have a COVID test before every treatment.

Being with the lab nurses for this extended period of time has given Tim and me the chance to build relationships with them. When we walk in the door, different ones call us by name to say hello, as I am sure they do with all patients. They speak as they walk by the cubby. They remember things about our family and ask about them.

The feeling of comfort that this personalization brings is great on many levels but especially since Tim can no longer go into the cancer center with me because of visitation restrictions. Before the restrictions were in place, he was with me at every treatment. However, like I said before, currently he does not let these rules stop him from being close to me. He may not be allowed in the cancer center, but I can count on him to be sitting outside my window in his lounge chair so he will be near me during my treatment.

No matter the weather, you will find Tim outside of Deanna's chemo window. This is what true love looks like.

Not only do the nurses in the lab take care of me, but there are other people who are part of the team that deserve a shout-out as well. Before COVID hit, we had volunteers who were also there to share a smile and to make sure we were all comfortable. They would bring us warm blankets, pillows, socks, snacks, and drinks. They even served us lunch, which was nice. Anything we needed or wanted, they would get for us. Along with these volunteers who were there daily, there were two men who would bring their therapy dogs in from time to time for us to love on and help us to relax.

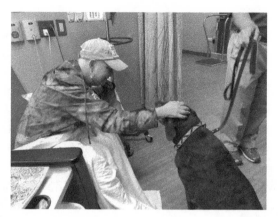

A furry visitor stops by to bring a smile to Deanna's face.

Another person I want to give a shout-out to that was part of my lab visits was our wonderful art teacher, Andrea. She would come around while we were getting treatments and do projects with us one-on-one. I am a crafty person, so this was right up my alley! She taught me to use watercolors and alcohol ink. We made cards and other projects. In addition to her lab visits, she scheduled outside art classes for cancer patients.

For art therapy during chemo, Andrea is showing Deanna ways to make different Valentine's Day cards.

Because of the virus, the hospital had to stop the volunteer program plus the art classes. They were a big part of our lab visits. Hopefully they will be back soon. I really miss their sweet smiles and kindness.

With the volunteers being gone, who do you think picked up the responsibility of making sure we are comfortable with blankets, pillows, and the rest of the goodies? Yep! Our nurses. They go over and beyond what is expected of them to make sure each of us is cared for and happy.

The awesomeness of the nurses continues on the oncology floor of the hospital. Believe me, I have been admitted enough times to get to know several of them. Even though they have many patients to take care of at the same time, they have always made me feel special and that they were there for me. I know they are overworked, so to be able to go from room to room with a smile on their face and love in their heart says a lot.

In all areas of the cancer center, our nurses rock! Tim and I are both grateful for the love they have shown us.

Every time I have to go to the emergency room, I know they are going to admit me because of my medical history—or at least that has been my experience so far. The nurses who work in there have always been kind too; however, because of the setting, there is no time to build relationships with them. So even though there are nurses there with me, I get scared. Scared of what is happening. Scared of a new diagnosis. Scared of not having Tim there with me anymore. Just scared. Truth? It would be so easy to give up but that is not happening with this girl. Giving up is not in my vocabulary.

I am so used to having Tim with me holding my hand through it all that it is really tough without him. It is so much easier when he is with me. I was about to type that it is really tough to be there alone, but do you know what? I am not alone. Ever. That is because God is there with me. He will never leave me. Because I cling to Him, He calms the fears I have. He gives me strength I need. He is the reason I make it. And you know what? The hospital cannot keep Him away. Nope! They cannot put restrictions on Him!

Even with the multiple challenges we have had to face, you may find this hard to believe and possibly a bit strange, but believe it or not, I am happy with my life right now. I am truly happy even though I am fighting a battle constantly.

Does being happy with my life mean I like being sick? Of course not! Do I enjoy going through all the junk I have had to endure? Absolutely not!

I do, however, love the peace that my relationship with Jesus Christ brings me. I love the closeness that I feel to Him. I love that He brings me joy. I love that our relationship has grown so much stronger through the challenges I have faced and the thankfulness for my blessings.

That is it. What is? The relationship. It is all about the relationship. Everything. No matter with who or what you are involved in, it is all about the relationship.

Think about it. Whether you are at home, church, work, school, a party, wherever, it is about the relationship you have with the people around you.

It is the same with Jesus. It is about the relationship you have with Him. The true relationship—your trust in Him, your faith in Him, your belief that He takes care of things in His timing, the belief that He has a reason for everything, the belief that He is always by your side and will never leave you for any reason. Your relationship with Him grows just like it does with a family member or friend. It does not happen overnight.

I would like to share the story of how my relationship with Jesus started. My mama always took me to church from the time I was born. One Sunday morning, when I was either five or six, I was helping my aunt in the nursery during the sermon. I am not too sure how much "helping" I was actually doing at that age, but I know I was at the right place at the right time.

Deanna is thankful, grateful, and blessed to have
been raised by her Christian mama, Nancy.

Thankfully there was a speaker in there from where we could hear the service. Of course, at that age and the fact that I was playing with the kids in the nursery, I am pretty sure I was not listening to too much of the sermon. But undoubtedly, I heard enough that I knew Jesus was speaking to my heart.

When the preacher was finished preaching, he gave an altar call to the congregation. I remember wanting to go to the altar. I remember the tug on my heart.

As I was trying to leave the nursery, a big, tall, dark-haired man was blocking the doorway.

"Where are you going?"

"To the altar."

"You're too little to go to the altar."

I walked around him and headed straight to the front of the church. It was that day that I asked Jesus to forgive me of my sins and to come into my heart. It was that day that I became a Christian. It was that day that I started my true relationship with Him.

I normally listened when adults spoke to me, but that morning, I did not listen to the man in the doorway, and I am glad I did not. I knew what I wanted, and I was going to make it happen. Children are not too young to ask Jesus into their heart.

Growing up as a Christian helped prepare me for the challenges that came my way, whether it was with school, friends, work, the teenage years, college days, marriage, being a mama—whatever I faced, Jesus has always been with me.

It was not until I was much older that my relationship grew deeper with Him. I had always been close to Jesus, but as I grew older, I learned that there was so much more than I ever realized.

Many years ago, I had come to what I considered one of the lowest points in my life. I was not the happy-go-lucky person I had always been. I was so overwhelmed and felt like I just could not get it all together. I felt like I was giving and giving but it was never enough. I was not liking me very much.

What could I do? How could I get back to being me? I was tired of feeling that way. I wanted my old self back.

One day, I went into a local bakery, and there stood my answer. A lady had on a shirt that read "Too Blessed to Be Stressed."

That was it! What had I been doing? I had all these blessings around me, yet I was letting the negative stuff in my life blind me from seeing what was right in front of my face. I stood there and cried. Yes, right there in the bakery, I stood and cried.

It was at that exact point that I decided my life would change. I decided then and there to find the blessings in everything that happened to me. No matter what, I chose to look for the good in all things.

This started me talking to Jesus more—just like a friend. It helped me get back on track with our relationship that I had gotten slack with. I am very grateful for that day in the bakery because, believe me, it started preparing me for what I am currently facing.

Looking for the good things happening in my life these past few years has kept me positive. I needed that strengthened relationship with Jesus. It would have been extremely easy to let myself go, but with Him by my side and a positive spirit, I have made it through many tough situations. He will never leave me. He will never leave any of us.

I was talking to my friend Lisa about my story. I told her that I wanted the focus to be on what God has done for me, not on me, because I am not special; He is.

She disagreed.

"You are special. We're all special because we're all children of God."

You know what? She was right. We are all special. Every single one of us. You, me, all of us. He loves us all, no matter what we have done in our lives, and will take care of our needs.

I have heard people say that God does not answer their prayers. He *does* answer our prayers—all of them. It may just not be the answer you want or in the time frame you want.

Remember, it is in His timing. His timing is perfect. Not yours or mine, but His.

Think about it. I have been going through all these different illnesses, starting with cancer, for going over four years. Whoever thought this crazy journey would last this long?

Would anybody want to go through what I am going through for as long as I have been dealing with it? Absolutely not. However, I truly believe that when it is the right time, His timing, I will be healed.

How can I still say that after all that is taking place in my life? How can I be so sure? My answers are easy.

My faith.

My relationship with Jesus.

I am thankful to say that I am still growing in both of these areas every day of my life, the same way you can.

As you have read earlier in my story, I truly believe Jesus has a reason for everything that happens—whether we think it is good or bad, He has a reason. I mean, really, who would think cancer is good? Surely not me. But when I was diagnosed, I had two choices.

I could have felt sorry for myself, given up, and let it take me down, or I could have chosen to find the positive in it and fight with everything I had. I chose the latter. Because of my relationship with Jesus, I knew He had a plan for me. I just had to figure it out. What is the positive that I found? That I get to share His love and the miracles He has done in my life. I have grown closer to Him than I ever imagined. Am I perfect? No way—nowhere close, and I do not claim to be, but I do try to live according to His will.

How do I know His plans and His will?

I pray and ask Him. I have a personal relationship with Him.

About praying. Some people think a prayer to Jesus has to be full of thees and thous, formal words that scare some people away from prayer because they don't know "how to do it right." Please believe me when I say there is no "right" or "wrong" way to pray.

Look at it this way.

Is this the way you would talk to your friend?

Jesus is your friend.

Is this the way you would talk to your father?

Ultimately, He is your Father.

Nope. Not me. I do not use formal words with my friends, and I did not use them with my daddy when he was alive.

If you hear me pray, you may think I am starting off like a kid, and that is okay. All of my prayers start off with "Dear Jesus." I pray just like I speak, as if I am having a normal conversation with Him. In reality, that is what it is. A conversation. What is important is what you are saying, not how you are saying it. Let it flow freely. He knows your heart.

Personally, I talk to Jesus throughout the day. Yes, I pray to Him, but it also may be a simple "thank you" for the gifts He places in my life—my family, my friends, the beautiful sunshine, the rain to help plants grow.

In life, it is too easy to let whatever is happening around you get you down. When you try to take on the world by yourself, that is what happens. Even worse, it is hard to dig yourself out of the hole you put yourself in.

Who wants to live a life like that? Not me! I am guessing you do not either. The great thing is that you do not have to!

One thing I know for sure is that God is still in the miracle-making business! If you have any doubts about that, look at my life. *I am a miracle.* A lot of people have told me that, including doctors and nurses.

One last "funny" from Dr. Miller, my oncologist.

"Your cancer is dumb."

"What?"

"Your cancer is just dumb. It is too dumb to know that it was supposed to take your life a long time ago. We are just going to let it keep being dumb and we're going to keep on keeping you alive!"

She is such a hoot!

Dumb cancer? We will claim it because it makes us laugh, but the real fact is that my Jesus has worked miracles time and again in my life for over four years now. It is all Him.

What He is doing for me, He will do for you too.

Family Photo Credit: Whitney Dena' Photography

About the Author

Irresistible Portraits
by Karen Goforth

Deanna has earned her National Board of Professional Teaching Standards Certification in Early Childhood, her master of arts degree, and bachelor of science degree, both in Early Childhood Education, from Wingate University, and her Academically and Intellectually Gifted Certification. Her awards include being one of four state finalists for the North Carolina Association of Educators' Terry Sanford Award for Creative Teaching, Teacher of the Year for her elementary school, and the Hilbish Ford Teacher of the Month.

Now retired after thirty years in the classroom, Deanna enjoys spending time with her husband, children, and grandchildren, whether it is being at the beach, in the mountains, playing games, camping, or going to dinner together. She is a volunteer with Camp LUCK (Lucky Unlimited Cardiac Kids), which is a residential camp for children with heart disease. She also volunteered at YMCA Camp Cherokee for over twenty years.

Deanna enjoys traveling, writing, being outside, camping, and crafting.

CPSIA information can be obtained
at www.ICGtesting.com
Printed in the USA
LVHW041232160621
690357LV00003B/265

9 781636 923895